THE LITTLE BOOK
OF ICELANDIC

ALDA SIGMUNDSDÓTTIR

THE LITTLE BOOK
OF ICELANDIC

ON THE IDIOSYNCRASIES,
DELIGHTS, AND SHEER TYRANNY
OF THE ICELANDIC LANGUAGE

LITTLE BOOKS
PUBLISHING

TABLE OF CONTENTS

Introduction

Icelandic is a complicated language. It's a bloody mess grammatically, a nightmarish mishmash of inflected nouns, verbs, adjectives and pronouns, corresponding to four different cases, three different noun genders, moods, voices and constructions, plus any number of exceptions and rules that seem completely arbitrary, and very often are.

As a matter of fact, the Icelandic language is a lot like the Icelandic people. In my casual study of the Icelanders over the years I have been able to ascertain only one thing: they are impossible to pin down because they are full of paradoxes. The moment you think you know one thing about them ("they are so cosmopolitan!") the polar opposite will suddenly pop out at you ("oh but they're so provincial, forever trying to keep up with the Joneses"). The Icelandic language, meanwhile, has at its core a crazy paradox: this impossibly difficult grammar, and an endearingly prosaic, almost naive way of cobbling together vocabulary.

So perhaps the Icelanders love Icelandic so much because it mirrors the essence of their collective souls. And love it they do. Whenever someone conducts one of those "what is it that defines us as a nation" surveys, at the top of the list is usually "our mother tongue". Note: not "the language" or "Icelandic", but "our mother tongue". You see, when the Icelanders start talking about Icelandic they get all highbrow and poetic. Indeed, a popular sobriquet for the language is *okkar ástkæra ylhýra*, which literally means "our beloved and gentle". Need I say more?

This book is not about the technicalities of Icelandic. It is not a book that will help you learn the language, or make sense of Icelandic grammar. It is not even a book that will help you order a beer in a pub. (Don't worry. You can use English for that.) Rather it is an overly ambitious and rather inadequate attempt to present how the very essence of the Icelandic people and their culture is reflected in the language.

That nature is in large part shaped by the fight to survive in adverse circumstances - a harsh climate, a beautiful yet unforgiving landscape, geographical isolation, and intense poverty. One of the greatest revelations to me after I started working on this book is how those things tend to crystallise in the idioms and proverbs of the language. They reveal the things that cut to the heart of the nation and so I have paid special attention to them. I also discovered that Icelandic has such a great many idioms and proverbs that I only managed to cover a fraction. I am now starkly aware of how much the Icelanders like to express themselves in allusions.

Before I proceed I should warn speakers of American English that punctuation is placed outside of quotation marks throughout this book. This is on purpose, because I decided to go with British English. Hence some words may look misspelled to you, while they probably look correct to those who live across the pond. Conversely, I have sometimes used American terms for things ("sweater" springs to mind) that may look odd to the British speakers but which look perfectly OK to me. Blame it on my Canadian upbringing, if you will.

I also had some feedback concerning the Icelandic terms in this book - specifically that non-native speakers were interested in knowing how they are pronounced. This presented a bit of a dilemma. In the end I decided on this: to record the various terms, and to post the audio file on my website under the URL aldasigmunds.com/audiofile. So if you read something in this book and are curious about how it sounds, you will find the answer there.

Finally, a cursory warning: this book contains profanity in places, so if you're sensitive about that sort of thing you may want to read it with one eye closed. Consider yourselves warned.

A brief, brief history of Icelandic

Before I start dissecting I should probably provide a bit of background. Icelandic, as you may know, is a Nordic language, which makes it a subgroup of the Germanic languages. By virtue of this you might think that we would automatically be able to understand our Danish, Swedish and Norwegian brethren (the Finns, of course, are out in the linguistic stratosphere somewhere) and that they, in turn, would be able to understand us.

This is not so.

Iceland was settled by Norwegian Vikings in the 9th century AD (and, as it happens, by the Irish slaves they kidnapped en route, but nobody ever talks about that). The language spoken by these Vikings formed the basis of Icelandic, and the two languages - Old Norwegian and Icelandic - remained very similar until around the 14th century. From that point on Norwegian started to change due to external influences, but given that Iceland was a tad out of the way geographically and Icelanders generally weren't skipping off to the mainland whenever they felt like it, Icelandic remained trapped in a sort of linguistic time capsule. Due to their isolation the Icelanders have quite unwittingly maintained their primitive, arbitrary grammar, and are therefore the etymological equivalent of a primal tribe somewhere in Africa.

Back in those days people weren't too concerned with the intricacies of case and inflection and all the things that make grammar so complex. In fact, they probably didn't even have a word for "grammar". They just talked in some random Neanderthal fashion about the things they wanted to talk about. Over time and with expanded use of a language the rough edges got polished off and people's verbal expressions became smooth and streamlined - much as we see in English, at least grammatically speaking. But not so with Icelandic.

That said, let me now backpedal and declare that Icelandic does, in fact, have a linguistic sibling, and that linguistic sibling is Faroese, the language of the Faroe Islands. The Faroes are located southeast of Iceland and were, like Iceland, originally settled by Vikings. While Icelanders don't have a particularly easy time conversing with other Nordic nationals, unless they have learned their languages in school, they *can* converse reasonably easily with the Faroese. Like Icelandic, the Faroese language remained isolated throughout the centuries and did not absorb many external influences. So the Icelanders and the Faroese essentially occupy adjacent linguistic bubbles with enough overlap that they can actually understand one another - at least if they don't speak terribly fast.

Fun false friends

But here's the thing: to both the Icelanders and the Faroese, the other language often sounds like a slightly naive version of their own language. Its various terms can also seem borderline rude - enough to send the more juvenile among us into a fit of giggles.

Take for example the phrase *gildur limur*. In Faroese, gildur means "valid", whereas in Icelandic it means "thick". Limur, meanwhile, means "member" in Faroese (as in, member of an association), whereas in Icelandic it means "penis". So gildur limur means "a valid member of an organisation" in Faroese, and "thick penis" in Icelandic.

The same phrase in Icelandic, however, would be *fullgildur meðlimur* - slightly different, but close enough so that all Icelanders can figure out what gildur limur actually means to our Faroese friends.

This is but one example of many.

I don't know of any similar examples in Faroese (I'm not a linguistic insider, obviously) but I truly hope they have them, and that they sit snickering and grinning at our language in the same way we do at theirs.

All my kinder!

On the subject of "false friends" - words that are similar but mean different things in different languages - I am reminded of a story about an Icelandic farmer who went to Germany.

The word for "children" in German is *kinder*, as in Kindergarten. The word for "sheep" in Icelandic is *kindur*.

Very similar, as you can plainly see.

So this Icelandic farmer meets a German, who very genially asks him: "How many children (kinder) do you have?"

The Icelander replies, "Oh about 200".

The German is understandably taken aback, and exclaims, "Oh my! Is it not difficult to take care of so many?"

"Nah," says the Icelander. "If it gets to be too much we just slaughter a few and eat them."

But I digress.

Ísl-enska

It is pretty easy to geek out on Icelandic and English etymology if you like that sort of thing, finding ways in which the two were alike before they diverged and Icelandic floated off to stagnate in its own lexical bubble. Both Icelandic and English are part of the Indo-European language family and even share a secondary branch on the linguistic tree, as both are Germanic languages. This common origin can be perceived in many Icelandic and English words today, such as house = *hús* and book = *bók*, to name just two.

Other words demonstrate well how Icelandic stalled while English evolved. For example, changes occurred in English whereby a term that once meant something general became narrowed down to mean one thing in particular. Linguists call this "semantic narrowing".

An example is the word "hound", which used to mean any dog, but which today is a specific term meaning hunting dog. In Icelandic, meanwhile, the word *hundur*, an etymological brother to "hound", still means any dog. Another example: "meat" used to mean any type of food in English, but today is used to talk about the flesh of an animal. In Icelandic the word *matur*, from the same root as "meat", still means any type of food.

Old English is, of course, unrecognisable to modern English speakers for the most part. To Icelanders, on the other hand, it often seems vaguely familiar. I once taught English for a summer in England, and one of the other teachers told me about an Icelandic student he had in one of his classes. He had shown the class a BBC documentary about the origins of English, and in one scene there was a person who spoke a dialect from the north of England that had changed very little since the Vikings had invaded back in the eight century AD. (The Vikings then continued on to Iceland.) The punch line of the story was that the Icelandic student in the class was able to understand the ancient dialect in the documentary, whereas the English speakers were not. To them it sounded completely alien.

Perhaps it is no wonder then that the Icelandic word for English is "enska" while Icelandic (in Icelandic) is "ísl-enska".

A cursory mention of grammar

I know I said this book wasn't about grammar, but I have to give a wee sample just to illustrate what those intrepid souls who try to study Icelandic are up against.

Full disclosure: I am not an expert in Icelandic grammar by any stretch. I barely have a clue what I am talking about. And you know what? Most Icelanders don't have a clue, either. Ask them about Icelandic grammar and they'll stare at you blankly for a minute before shrugging their shoulders, shaking their heads, and declaring that they really don't know - they just speak it the way they learned it.

That said ~

Icelandic has four grammatical cases. Each verb, noun and adjective is inflected (read: changes) according to the case being used. Let's take a look at the noun *hestur* (horse) which for some reason became the default word for illustrating this concept in Icelandic grammar teaching.

HESTUR

Nominative case: *Hér er hestur*

Accusative case: *Um hest*

Dative case: *Frá hesti*

Genitive case: *Til hests*

Translation:

Here is a horse

About a horse

From a horse

To a horse

Plural

Nominative: *Hér eru hestar*

Accusative: *Um hesta*

Dative: *Frá hestum*

Genitive: *Til hesta*

Translation:

Here are horses

About horses

From horses

To horses

As you can see, the English noun does not inflect (change), and the plural is formed simply by adding an -s. However, if you are speaking Icelandic, you pretty much have to determine a) which case you are using for what you want to say and b) which form of the noun you are going to use.

If you have grown up with the language, you'll have learned this by osmosis. If you have not, you're kind of out on the raging ocean without an oar - to adapt a well-known English idiom to Icelandic circumstances.

Incidentally, *hestur* is one of the easy nouns. You also have not-so-easy nouns, like the irregular ones. Let's just take ... oh, the word *alda*. (Yes I know that is my name, but it is also a regular old irregular noun that means "wave" - as in, wave on the sea.) I'll omit the names of the cases - they are the same as above.

ALDA
Hér er alda
Um öldu
Frá öldu
Til öldu

Plural:
Hér eru öldur
Um öldur
Frá öldum
Til alda

You see? *It changes completely*. Into a whole different word. Apparently for no logical reason other than to mess with you.

As for the verbs, I'm not even going to go there. Suffice it to say that they govern the cases of the nouns, adjectives and pronouns. Also that they are all conjugated according to classes defined as weak or strong, and each weak or strong group has three sub-groups. Also there is no rhyme or reason governing which verb belongs to which class or group. *You just have to know.*

He she it

Before I fully abandon the grammar malarkey, I must briefly mention genders. Noun genders.

If you know languages like German and French you will already be familiar with nouns having genders that have nothing to do with the actual gender of the thing. After all, how can a coffee pot (*kaffikanna*) be a "she", a coffee cup (*kaffibolli*) a "he", and a coffee shop (*kaffihús*) an "it"? Makes no sense.

Why is this important? Well, because the gender of the noun determines how it is declined in a sentence. The noun

will have a different ending depending on whether it is masculine, feminine or neuter. If you want to learn Icelandic properly, you have to memorise the gender for *every single noun*.

And before you ask, no - the noun genders are not the same as in other languages. If you know German, say, and think you have the gender thing pegged, I fear I have to disappoint you. Icelandic nouns will not necessarily have the same gender as German nouns. Or French nouns. Or any other nouns that use the same form.

Throughout this book I will give frequent examples of Icelandic words, and sometimes they will change from one sentence to another. This is because they will be describing different genders. For example, the adjective *fallegur* (beautiful) will change according to whether it is describing a masculine noun (in which case it will be fallegur), a feminine noun (*falleg*) or a neuter noun (*fallegt*). Just so you know.

Women and men

Speaking of genders.

You know how they're always saying that Iceland has such great gender equality? That may be true to an extent, but even in Iceland patriarchal attitudes underpin things, which is most excellently reflected in the Icelandic language and the way those in charge choose to form it.

To wit: the noun "minister" in Icelandic is *ráðherra* (literally "ruling sir" ... no, I am not making this up) and it happens to be masculine. You refer to "he" the minister - and you do this even if the minister is a woman. Granted, there was a time when there were no women in government, so it is perhaps understandable that the noun should have started out in masculine form. However, when women *did* start to make inroads into this male-dominated territory they were simply dubbed ráðherra, the same as their male counterparts. This has stuck to this day.

The same is true of pretty much all professions that were once traditionally male. For instance the word for pilot in Icelandic is *flugmaður* ("flying man" ... did I already mention the Icelanders' adorable way of constructing vocab?), and a female pilot is called - correct! - *also* "flying man".

On the other side of the equation you have professions that used to be traditionally female. Like nurse, for instance. In Icelandic, the word for nurse used to be *hjúkrunarkona* ("nursing woman"), until some men came along who wanted to enter this traditionally female profession.

So do you think male nurses in today's Iceland are called "nursing women"? *Of course not.* When nurses started to become male, the name was changed to something more gender-neutral so those poor males that entered the profession didn't have to cope with the humiliation of being called "women". So now hjúkrunarkona has morphed into *hjúkrunarfræðingur* ("nursing specialist"). The same applies to *skúringakona* ("cleaner"), now *ræstitæknir* ("cleaning technologist"), *flugfreyja* ("stewardess"), now *flugliði* or *flugþjónn* (flight attendant/flight server - though female flight attendants are usually still called flugfreyja), and more.

So you see, in Iceland women may be men, but men are certainly not women.

Old letters,
strange sounds

The Icelandic alphabet is a Latin alphabet, like the English one, but it comprises 32 letters, as opposed to 26 in English. While that sounds like a lot of extra letters, many of those are actually made up of vowels with diacritics (little accents above them) that serve to change their sounds. For instance, "a" is pronounced *ah*, whereas "á" is pronounced *ow*. Similarly "i" is pronounced *ih* whereas "í" is pronounced *ee*.

Yet it is not all down to diacritics - Icelandic also has three characters that are pretty unfamiliar to English speakers: þ, ð and æ.

Þ is called "thorn" in both Icelandic and English, and in Icelandic is pronounced "thoddn". It used to exist in Old English, Old Norse and the Gothic languages, but over time it became obsolete - except in Icelandic. The sound it represents is a "th" sound, as in, well, "thorn". Given that þ is relatively unfamiliar to most people, many foreigners, on seeing it for the first time, are inclined to pronounce it "P". So Þingvellir National Park becomes "Pingvellir National Park"

- something that makes most Icelanders giggle uncontrollably because, frankly, it sounds completely wacko.

Ð, meanwhile, used to exist in Old English, Middle English and ... wait for it ... *Elfdalian*. Yes, a language by that adorable name actually exists and is spoken by around 2,000 people in a valley called Övdaln in northern Sweden. Today, ð still exists in Icelandic, Faroese and Elfdalian, and is called eth. The sound it makes is very similar to the thorn, except that the "th" sound is softer, as in "there". No word in Icelandic ever starts with ð, so the upper case Ð is only used when writing words in all-uppercase letters.

Then there is Æ/æ, which in English is called aesc, or ash. It used to exist in Old English but has become obsolete except where folks wish to retain some kind of archaic spelling (Encyclopædia Britannica springs to mind). Æ is pronounced exactly as an English speaker would pronounce "I".

A handful of letters are conspicuous by their absence in the Icelandic alphabet, specifically c, q, w and z.

The first three, c, q and w, have never existed there, which may account for the fact that Icelanders, when speaking English, almost always get "v" and "w" mixed up. They don't hear the difference unless they make a concerted effort to do so, and will by default say "wery" instead of "very" and "grapewine" instead of "grapevine".

Z, on the other hand, used to be a part of Icelandic, but

was banished by decree back in the 1970s. Its crime? Merely that it could not be differentiated from "s" in Icelandic pronunciation, so it was basically useless. But the Icelanders have never been much for decrees and tend to regard them as mere guidelines - hence there are some die-hards that have stayed loyal to the "z" and absolutely refuse to oust it from their written correspondence. These include the newspaper Morgunblaðið that, at the time this is penned, still writes everything with a z, and commercial college Verzlunarskólinn, which insists on keeping the z in its name.

Truth be told, it is a little hard to see just why z was singled out and sent packing. After all, the letter i sounds exactly like y in written language, and í exactly like ý - but neither of those have been banished.

Which may just indicate that the prescriptive rules governing Icelandic are about as arbitrary as the Icelandic language they are supposed to regulate.

The disease and death of Icelandic

So who are the nebulous "they" that keep messing with the Icelandic language?

In most cases that would be the Icelandic Language Committee, whose job it is to advise the authorities on language-related business. The committee is appointed by the Minister of Culture and is, among other things, entrusted with ensuring that Icelandic remains pure and unsullied by making up new words whenever something appears that doesn't have an Icelandic name yet. So instead of taking, say, the word "computer", Icelandicising it, and calling it *kompjúter*, they made up the word *tölva*, which is composed of the words *tala* (number) and *völva* (prophetess). So the word for computer in Icelandic is, effectively, "prophetess of numbers".

This anxiety about the demise of the Icelandic language is not a new thing. Efforts to manually preserve it began as early as the 1100s when the first grammatical treatise, aptly named *The First Grammatical Treatise*, was released. This groundbreaking document essentially proposed the construction of a special Icelandic alphabet, derived from the Latin alphabet but adapted to incorporate all those special sounds the Icelanders made when they spoke, including the aforementioned thorn (þ). In the end its suggestions were not all adopted, but it turned out to be highly influential nonetheless.

Then in the 18th century, renowned explorer and writer Eggert Ólafsson penned a poem with the hair-raising title *Sótt og dauði íslenskunnar*, literally "The Disease and Death of Icelandic". There he likened the Icelandic language to a woman who is diseased and on the brink of death from being contaminated by too many foreign words. Granted, the poem was a little on the satirical side, yet with a serious undertone in which Eggert urged his fellow Icelanders to maintain the purity of their mother tongue.

Advice that they evidently took to heart since the whole idea of linguistic purism started to pick up momentum in the late 19th century, parallel to the independence movement. The formal regulation of the Icelandic language began in 1918, culminating in the establishment of the Icelandic Language Committee in 1965.

Say how?

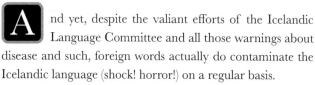

And yet, despite the valiant efforts of the Icelandic Language Committee and all those warnings about disease and such, foreign words actually do contaminate the Icelandic language (shock! horror!) on a regular basis.

In a moment I'm going to give you a list of a few English words that have entered the Icelandic language as slang in the last few years, and which have become established enough to occasionally appear in written Icelandic. The thing is, though, that they are inevitably written phonetically - that is, exactly how they sound to an Icelander, using the Icelandic alphabet.

So here is a brief pronunciation key. Brief, as in just the sounds the vowels make. Using those, see if you can figure out what English slang words appear below.

THE VOWEL SOUNDS OF ICELANDIC

A - ah

Á - ow

E - eh (as in bed)

É - ye

I - ih (as in ick)

Í - ee (as in eek)

O - o (as in bored)

Ó - oh

U - (no exact sound in English for this. The closest I can come is "burr" but even that's a shade off)

Ú - ooh

Y - the same as i

Ý - the same as í

Æ - I (as in "me")

Then there are the diphthongs:

ei - pronounced ay

au - no exact sound in English for this, either. The closest I can come is "oy".

Okay then!

The viruses

Below is a list of some common viruses in Icelandic today, those nasty bugs that are contaminating the lovely Icelandic language and leaving her diseased and on the brink of damnation. These are derived exclusively from English, from which the vast majority of Icelandic loanwords are taken. As I mentioned the words are transcribed phonetically into Icelandic, meaning they are written with Icelandic letters to sound like the word in English. Sometimes the words also have suffixes and suchlike attached to them, which makes them easier to inflect and thus causes them to infiltrate the Icelandic tongue in an even more insidious manner than they otherwise would.

If you get completely stumped, there is an answer key on page 156.

1. **Bömmer**
2. **Meika sens**
3. **Kræst**
4. **Fríkað**
5. **Dömpa**
6. **Stöffa**
7. **Kreisí**
8. **Sjitt**
9. **Bögg**
10. **Deit**
11. **Sánd**
12. **Djók**
13. **Sjokk**
14. **Plís**
15. **Djísus**
16. **Pein**
17. **Sækó**
18. **Brönsj**
19. **Gúgla**
20. **Osom**
21. **Tjilla**

Hatching new words

So how does the Icelandic Language Committee comes up with new words, or "neologisms" as they are called?

Basically there are five different ways. They are, in no particular order:

CREATING COMPOUND WORDS This would appear to be a party favourite, given that so many Icelandic words are constructed this way. Take the word *sjónvarp* (television), for instance. It is made up of the words *sjón* (sight) and *varp* (to project). So sjónvarp basically means "sight projector". Or take one that is completely outdated now but which I always thought was genius: *vasadiskó*, made up of the word *vasi* (pocket) and *diskó* (disco). "Pocket disco", the name for the now-obsolete Sony Walkman. A little party in your pocket.

TRANSLATING LOAN WORDS INTO ICELANDIC As we have established, the language committee is dead against adopting foreign words into Icelandic as-they-are. But they are not averse to adopting those very same words provided they are first translated into Icelandic, more or less verbatim. Some examples: *loftpúði* (airbag), made up of *loft* (air) and *púði* (cushion). *Heilapvottur* (brainwashing) made up of *heili* (brain) and *pvottur* (washing). *Sandkassi* (sandbox), made of *sandur* (sand) and *kassi* (box). And so on.

ADAPTING WORDS This ingenious method involves putting foreign loan words through the linguistic meat grinder to make them conform to those ridiculously complex Icelandic language conventions and rules. For good measure they are also phonetically adapted. Examples include *skáti* (derived from scout) and *gír* (derived from gear, as on a car). Another slightly far-removed example is the word *bíll* (car) taken from the Danish word *bil*, which in turn is shortened from the English "automobile".

REVIVING OLD SUFFIXES This means that suffixes that once were used to make new words but aren't any more are once again used to make new words. Example: the suffix *-ald*, which once upon a time was added to verbs to make new terms. For example, in the old days the word *rekald* (flotsam) was made from the verb *reka* (to float) and this -ald suffix. To-day the suffix -ald has been revived and is used to make new words such as *mótald* (modem), which is made from *móttaka* (reception) and -ald.

RECYCLING OLD WORDS The Icelanders are terrible at recycling stuff, but they're actually pretty good at recycling words. Here the lingo commit-tee reaches deep into Icelandic history to discover words that are no longer actively used, but which once upon a time had meaning. Probably the best known is *sími* (telephone) which originally meant "long thread". When the Icelanders were stuck for a name for "telephone" they thought of the wire needed to transport the voice and remembered that way back in yonder days there had been this word. So sími became the word for phone. Today, of course, we no longer have long threads that allow you to talk to your grandmother or auntie - we use cellular networks for that. So naturally the language committee had invent a word for cellphone or mo-bile phone and they didn't deliberate long - *farsími* was the word of the day, made up of the prefix *far-* (migratory) and sími - "migratory phone".

Neotechisms

G iven the mad influx of technology into our modern lives, the Language Committee has certainly had its nose to the grindstone coming up with neologisms. Here are a few random examples of new or new-ish terms for technology in Icelandic.

Snjallsími (smartphone), made up of *snjallur* (clever) and *sími* (telephone) = clever phone.

Spjaldtölva (tablet), derived from *spjald* (straight board) and *tölva* (computer) = straight board computer.

Hleðslutæki (charger), made from *hleðsla* (loading) and *tæki* (tool) = loading tool.

Rafbíll (electric car), made from *raf* (electricity) and *bíll* (car) = electric car.

Forrit (application), made from the prefix *for-* (pre-) and *rit* (writings) = pre-writings.

Smáforrit (app), made from *smár* (little) and *forrit* (program/application) = little application.

Þráðlaust (wireless), made from *þráður* (thread) and *laust* (without) = without thread.

Flakkari (external hard drive), made from the verb *flakka*, meaning "wander". *Flakkari* actually existed in Icelandic before it was assigned this particular new term, and meant (means) "vagabond" or "wanderer".

Fartölva (laptop), made from the prefix *far-* (to migrate) and *tölvu* (computer) = migrating computer.

Lesbretti (e-reader) made from *lesa* (read) and *bretti* (board) = reading board.

Amapóstur (spam), made from the old word *ama* (something that annoys), and *póstur* (post/mail) = mail that annoys.

That last one has never really caught on in Icelandic, mind. Spam is usually referred to either as simply "spam" or *ruslpóstur* - "trash mail". This happens occasionally - that a word that the Language Committee makes up just refuses to take hold. A personal favourite of mine that has not found favour with the Icelandic public is *loðber* (kiwi), made from *loðið* (furry) and *ber* (berry) = furry berry. It is simply referred to as kiwi. I guess "furry berry" was a bit too much for the otherwise linguistically obedient Icelanders to, er, swallow.

Secret language club

So we have established that Icelandic is a pain in the butt if you have to learn it manually. In fact, the sorry truth is that most foreign learners who begin to learn Icelandic as adults don't manage to master it fully. To do so you essentially have to "drink it in with your mother's milk", to borrow an Icelandic adage. And given that not many Icelanders exist in the world, it follows that there are not very many people who speak Icelandic. There are only about 350,000 fluent speakers of Icelandic worldwide, and of those, around 320,000 live in Iceland.

Now, if you are an Icelander and you are somewhere abroad with another Icelander this can come in tremendously handy. Basically we can blather on about whatever strikes our fancy with pretty much total confidence that we will not be understood. I cannot count the times I have sat on a subway conversing with my travel companion about that annoying person stuffing her face next to me, or the businessman dude with his fly open, or the adorable kid with the braids ... and they never know we're talking about them. It's like having your own secret language.

This does come with a proviso, though. There are certain places in the world where Icelanders tend to congregate and you cannot be sure that you're safe. For instance I would never talk disparagingly about the person in front of me who refuses to stand right on the escalator if I was in an H&M store. This is because a) if the person refuses to stand right on the escalator there is a good chance that they are Icelandic because Icelanders believe the rules don't apply to them, and b) if it is in an H&M store the chances are twice as good because Icelanders *adore* H&M. In fact they go on special shopping excursions abroad *just* to go to H&M. They make a beeline for H&M the moment they get off the plane, and they stuff their suitcase, the empty one they brought with them expressly for the purpose of going to H&M, full of H&M stuff.

Bottom line: an Icelander needs to be careful about what they say in Icelandic in an H&M store because people may be listening. And even if they are in "the club with the secret language", if there are too many of them around there's just no secret any more.

Danish to English

While secret language clubs are fun and all, there is a downside: the fact that hardly anyone understands Icelandic means that, well, hardly anyone understands us. And since no one speaks our language, we have to speak theirs.

Consequently language learning is given high priority in the Icelandic educational system. Children start learning languages early, anywhere from grades two to five - it varies from school to school.

Until a few years ago, Danish was the first language taught in school. This was a throwback to our colonial past, when Icelanders needed to speak Danish to be able to converse with their overlords. I'm no expert, but it seems to me that it took an inordinate length of time for Icelandic authorities to figure out that teaching Danish as no. 1 foreign language was a complete time warp. The whole world was madly learning English, and for a good reason - it is used as lingua franca practically everywhere and is a whole lot more useful than Danish, with all due respect.

Anyway, sometime in the 1990s someone finally woke up and smelled the 21st century, priorities were revised, and now Icelandic elementary schools teach English first, Danish second. Other languages such as German, French, Spanish, Chinese, Japanese are added to the mix in succeeding years and taught as electives. The Scandinavian languages continue to be perennially popular, though, because despite everything there is a lot of Nordic cooperation that goes on, and many jobs require fluency in English and one Scandinavian language, in addition to Icelandic.

All in all, the general sentiment in Iceland tends to be that the more languages you speak, the more opportunities await you - and the tourism boom in recent years has certainly done nothing to dissuade that.

The Day of the Icelandic Tongue

I have mentioned the love and regard that the Icelanders have for their language, and lest anyone is still in doubt, I present to you: Dagur íslenskrar tungu.

Dagur íslenskrar tungu, literally "Day of the Icelandic Tongue", is a special day given over to the celebration of the Icelandic language. Not coincidentally it falls on November 16th each year, which was the birthday of one of Iceland's most beloved poets, Jónas

Hallgrímsson (1807-1845). He was sort of like the Icelandic Shakespeare, but without the cryptic language.

On Dagur íslenskrar tungu, various events are staged throughout the land. Most of them, it has to be said, are completely lacklustre - public officials visiting children's nursery schools to listen to the kiddies sing in their beautiful mother tongue, awards being handed out at stuffy ceremonies to some Icelander or other who is deemed to have enriched the language through their work, the Ministry of Culture urging all Icelanders to draw their Icelandic flag to full mast in celebration of their language.

In my opinion, the best activities on or around the Day of the Icelandic Tongue are competitions that are sometimes launched to find Icelandic neologisms for English-language words that despite the best efforts of the language police committee have managed to sneak into the language. The reason for their enthusiastic adoption by the common people is usually that there are no Icelandic words that adequately convey their meaning. You see, while there are words in Icelandic that cannot be translated into English because it fails to catch the nuances of meaning, the reverse is also true.

Here are a few English-language words that have made the list in recent years, along with the phonetic Icelandic spelling and also the closest Icelandic equivalent (the one that simply won't stick because it just doesn't fully express the idea, or just doesn't sound right).

Word & phonetic spelling	Closest Icelandic equivalent & meaning
casual - *kasúal*	*afslappað* - relaxed
crossover - *krossóver*	no equivalent
date (as in appointment) - *deit*	*stefnumót* - convergent meeting
fusion - *fjúsjón*	*bræðingur* - something that has been melted together
outlet - *átlet*	*útsöluverslun* - sale shop
to skateboard - *skeita*	*renna sér á rúllubretti* - to slide oneself on a rolling board
to surf (the web) - *sörfa*	*vafra* - browse
trendsetter - *trendsetter*	*tískufrömuður* - fashion innovator
wannabe - *vannabí*	*eftirherma* - mimicker

So you see - there are definitely times when only the English slang word will do.

Which is the prettiest of them all

In the last few years, Dagur íslenskrar tungu has also become a popular occasion for running polls to find the most beautiful word in the Icelandic language.

The most recent of these, conducted by the University of Iceland in 2013, was even more ambitious than its forerunners. It divided the nominations and voting into three different age groups, to see which word was favoured by which group. Below are the results of the poll, which selected the top three words in each age category. I've translated these wherever possible (it isn't always).

IN THE ADULT AGE GROUP (PEOPLE BORN BEFORE 1987)

1. *Ljósmóðir*

Meaning: Midwife

Verbatim translation: Light mother

(*ljós* = light, *móðir* = mother)

Ljósmóðir is a perennial favourite and tends to be at the top, or near the top, of most polls of this nature.

2. *Bergmál*

Meaning: Echo

Verbatim translation: Language of the mountains

(*berg* = rock, *mál* = language)

3. *Sindrandi*

Meaning: Shimmering, but with a much more expansive nuance. From the published poll results: "This word is clear and without artifice. It describes the magic world of Iceland; winter calm with crackling frost, the dancing lights of the night [the northern lights], morning dew in the calm of the mountains, a quivering horizon at sunset ... to name just a few."

Verbatim translation: Not possible

IN THE YOUNG ADULT AGE GROUP (BORN 1988 TO 1997)

1. *Hugfanginn*

Meaning: Fascinated

Verbatim translation: Captured by your mind

(*hugur* = mind, *fangi* = prisoner)

2. *Fiðringur*

Meaning: [Having] the jitters

Verbatim translation: Not possible, but takes from the word *fiður* = feathers. The meaning, in essence, is "feathers tickling your insides".

3. *Seigla*

Meaning: Toughness, tenacity and resolve, all rolled into one word. Or as one of the voters in the poll commented, "An unendingly beautiful word that describes limitless power".

Verbatim translation: Not possible

IN THE YOUNGEST AGE GROUP, BORN AFTER 1998, it would seem that the top-place words cannot be separated from the reasons behind their selection. There was commentary from unnamed voters accompanying each word, and by way of explanation I have included those as they appear on the Most Beautiful Word website (fegurstaordid.hi.is):

1. *Spékoppar*

Meaning: Dimples

Verbatim translation: Mischievous fun pots

(*spé* = mischievous fun, *koppar* = pots)

Commentary: "Spékoppar are beautiful. Also, it is fun to say spékoppar because it sounds so strange."

2. Einstök

Meaning: Unique

Verbatim translation: One single (*ein* = one, *stök* = single)

Commentary: "We all need to be praised sometimes, or to know that someone loves us. I think the word einstök is the perfect form of praise. It is such a warm word. It feels great to tell someone: You are einstök. Everyone is einstök, each in their own way."

3. Mamma

Verbatim translation: Mom

Meaning: Mom

Commentary: "Mother: 'Why do you think the word mamma is beautiful?' Son: 'Because you're my mother.' At which the mother melted." (Aw!)

Uglypoll

In the introduction to this book, I mentioned one thing intrinsic to the national character of the Icelanders: paradox.

Take for instance how they can have this terribly highbrow, almost reverential attitude towards their language, and at the same time be profoundly uncomfortable with anything that is overly sentimental or melodramatic.

So in response to the "most beautiful word in the Icelandic language hallelujah!" survey, it comes as little surprise that two guys should take it upon themselves to run a corresponding "the ugliest word in the Icelandic language" poll. Just to offer some comic relief, you understand. The veneration was becoming a tad too heavy.

The "ugly word" poll was, suitably enough, run on Facebook - that platform of the plebeians, so far removed from the exalted world of academic refinement (on paper, anyway). The public was invited to submit nominations for the ugliest word, and a grand total of 630 submissions were received, of which fifteen made the long list. The ultimate winners were voted upon by way of Facebook likes.

And so, hot on the heels of the "most beautiful word" results, I give you the three ugliest words in the Icelandic language, in reverse order, as determined by said poll.

3. *Líkþorn*
Verbatim translation: Corpse-dry
Meaning: Corn (as in, on your foot)
Sure, corns are a pain in the butt (albeit rarely - more commonly a pain in the foot) but associating them with a dried-up corpse is a little extreme, don't you think? This slightly grotesque word takes third place as the ugliest word in the Icelandic language.

2. *Mótþróaþrjóskuröskun*
Verbatim translation: Defiant Stubbornness Disorder
Official translation: Oppositional Defiant Disorder
It is hard to believe that this is actually a word, such is its convoluted length. Clearly whoever made it up saw no reason to split it into the three distinct parts that make up its meaning, opting instead to ram them together into a single abomination. Oppositionaldefiantdisorder is the second-ugliest word in the Icelandic language.

1. *Geirvarta*
Verbatim translation: Spear wart
Meaning: Nipple

Geir is an ancient word for spear. *Varta* is ... wart. This is one of the most glaring examples of Icelandic prosaicness, the jubilant triumph of the banal over the poetic. Definitely a very ugly word, and absolutely deserving of its victory.

OTHER NOTABLE RUNNERS-UP ... and yes, these are actual words, actually used by actual Icelanders in normal conversations - that is, if a conversation about necrophiliacs, scavengers and endometriosis can be considered normal:

Hrææta
Verbatim translation: Carcass eater
Meaning: Scavenger

Náriðill
Verbatim translation: Corpse fucker
Meaning: Necrophiliac

Legslímuflakk
Verbatim translation: Uterus slime wandering
Meaning: Endometriosis

Ófrísk

Verbatim translation: Un-fit (as in, not physically fit)

Meaning: Pregnant

Amazing alliteration

In Iceland, poets are regarded with a kind of awe. The very term *skáld* (poet) - in contrast to the more plebeian *rithöfundur* (writer) - is swathed in an otherworldly aura.

No doubt this reverence stems partly from the contribution made by the early Icelandic poets to Icelandic culture - and, indeed, world literature as a whole. Yet I am sure it is not just that. There is also the sheer skill required to write poetry in Icelandic. You see, not only does traditional Icelandic poetry have to rhyme, it also has to conform to a set of rules called *bragfræði* - prosody.

First, let's look at the rules. According to this system, a line of verse has to have two words beginning with the same consonant or a vowel, and the first word of the next line also has to begin with either that same consonant, or a vowel.

Confused? Here is an example, a poem called Sláttuvísa (Mowing Song) by Iceland's late great national poet Jónas Hallgrímsson:

Fellur **v**el á **v**elli
verkið karli sterkum,
syngur **e**nn á **e**ngi
eggjuð spík og rýkur
grasið **g**rænt á mosa,
grundin þýtur undir,
blómin **b**íða dóminn,
bítur ljár í skára.

You see, the first line has two words beginning with "v", and the next line of the verse also begins with "v". The third line has two words beginning with "e" and the first word of the next line begins with "e". And so on.

There are a couple of exceptions to this. One, the consonant "s" has its own rules, dictated by the letter that comes after the "s". So "st" only alliterates with "st", "sp" with "sp", and "sk" with "sk".

Two, a single-syllable word is permitted before the alliterated word in the second line, if needed.

If all that seems complicated, it was *way* worse in the old days. Traditional poetry had requirements for internal rhymes (where one word within a line or passage rhymes with another), various requirements regarding poetic feet, and more.

Now if that sounds like those folks in the old days were making things unduly difficult for themselves, consider: it was done not merely for fun, or to weed out the charlatans. Rather it was so that verses could be more easily remembered, as they were generally not written down. Epic poetry often constituted accounts of very real and important historical events, and people had to commit them to memory. And committing very long passages to memory was far easier if there were rhymes and alliterations and such, all throughout the poem.

Icelandic poetry more or less adhered to the prosody rules until around 1950, when poets began to buck the system and write experimental poetry. This poetry did not necessarily rhyme, it used new-fangled imagery, and was unconcerned with "the rules". Not that this entirely replaced the old way of doing things, though, and even today many people consider this form of poetry to be inferior to the traditional form.

And here is something remarkable: almost all translations of verse from other languages into Icelandic are still done in accordance with the rules of prosody. This includes Shakespearean text, songs in musicals and films, and more. Strangely these translators do not get awarded the same sort of respect that the poets do, even though they totally should. After all, it is hard enough to make up your own poetry while conforming to the rules, but when you have to force someone else's meaning into that form it becomes a task that is only for true aces to master.

The headscratchers

Every language has words that are hard to translate into other languages - often because the word, in the original, expresses something specific, even unique, to that nation or community. Here are a few random selections taken from our "beloved and gentle" that foreign visitors frequently find amusing - and sometimes bemusing.

❖ *Gluggaveður*
Verbatim translation: Window weather
Meaning: Weather that looks great from your window but is actually pretty nasty. Usually it means that the sun is shining brightly but it is miserably cold, most likely due to northerly winds from the Arctic.

❖ *Rassgat*
Verbatim translation: Asshole
Meaning: Adorable child
Yeah. We don't understand how this happened, either.

❖ Rokrassgat

Verbatim translation: Windy asshole

Meaning: A place that is really windy, usually on a perpetual basis.

It is tempting to associate this term with passing wind or similar, but there is really no connection - this is simply another inexplicable application of the word rassgat.

❖ Mín/minn

Verbatim translation: Mine

Meaning: You attach this little word as an endearment to the name of someone who is dear to you, especially a younger person or child. As in: "Alda mín, come eat your dinner," or "Gunni minn, go out and play!"

Incidentally, when this little word is used after your name by someone who is *not* close to you, its meaning immediately changes. This is particularly true if it is used by someone younger than you. That would, at best, be completely tactless, and at worst, seriously patronising - even if the user tried to wangle out of it by claiming it was said with the utmost affection. But trust me. If you are plugged into the cultural nuance of this word you know when it is an endearment, and when it is not. My advice to avoid any faux pas: never use it for someone who is not in your immediate family.

❖ *Kviðmágur*

Verbatim translation: Belly brother-in-law

Meaning: A man who has had sex with the same woman that another man has had sex with.

Yeah. There is a word for that. Two men who have had sex with the same woman are called "belly brothers-in-law". I know, it's gross. And thankfully it is not used very often - it's more like a joke. But still. It exists.

Plus a handful more

T hose words that are so difficult to translate often evoke for a native speaker a specific image or feeling filled with nuances and subtleties that cannot be communicated to a non-native speaker, even with the closest translated equivalent. Such words require explanations to get their full meaning across, and even that can be inadequate. Here are a handful in Icelandic that fall into this category, again chosen at random.

❖ Frekja

Verbatim translation: Doesn't exist

Meaning: Someone who is forceful and persistent when it comes to getting their way.

Usage: "That Gunna is such a frekja - she always insists on going first."

Sometimes a person, usually a woman, is dismissed as a frekja when they are simply demanding their rights. A man, in such an instance, would probably be called "assertive". This word does not always imply something negative - a person, often a child, can also be described as a frekja in a loving way, provided they are not overstepping boundaries *too* much.

❖ Hallærislegt

Verbatim translation: As in a downward-sloping year

Meaning: Something that is passé or uncool

Usage: "Can you believe he broke up with her on Facebook? That is *so* hallærislegt!"

Hallæri is actually a compound word - made of the word *halla*, meaning to lean, or slope downwards, and *æri*, which means year. A year that was a *hall-æri* was a year that was not prosperous. A lean year. And what happened in a lean year? People had less money to spend, and had to make do with old stuff that was not shiny and new. Today the word hallærislegt is used to describe things or behaviours that are second-rate or uncool, like the things people had to make do with in the scanty years.

❖ *Almennilegur*

Verbatim translation: In the manner of all men
Meaning: An individual who is described as almennilegur is someone who is nice, or personable.
Usage: "Stína's new boyfriend is so almennilegur, everybody likes him."

What I find interesting is that almennilegur is drawn from the words "all-men". So a person who is almennilegur is someone who is like everyone else - who is "not different" and therefore not threatening to the status quo. I should state here that I am not sure of the origins of the word, so these are just my own armchair musings. However, *if* this is the meaning behind the word, I find it interesting that "not different" came to be synonymous with "a nice, personable individual".

On the other hand, almennilegur could also have meant someone who treated all men equally, and was therefore a personable, courteous individual that people admired.

In addition to describing people, almennilegur can also mean "good and proper" as in, "that is an almennilegur hammer you're using" (meaning it exceeds expectations and does the job well), or "that is an almennilegt answer you gave him" (meaning you went above and beyond and really stuck it to him with your answer). We also say "That was *almennilegt*!" about an event or occurrence, which would simply mean that it was good, or noteworthy.

❖ *Stuð*

Verbatim translation: Electric shock

Meaning: The atmosphere whereby everyone is having an excellent time

Usage: Oh man, there was so much stuð at that party last night!

Stuð refers to the general mood or atmosphere that causes people to have a blast because they get caught up in it and cannot help but party their socks off. The related adjective is *í stuði*, literally "in stuð", which refers to the process of being affected by the stuð. At a party, or a concert, or wherever people are partying someone may shout at the top of their lungs: *Eru ekki allir í stuði?!* Meaning "Isn't everyone in the stuð!?" To which the proper response is to shout back YES!! at the top of your lungs and start dancing, headbanging or whatever.

Similarly, if you are feeling tired or inert and don't feel like doing something, whether it is partying, doing the dishes, or even watching your favourite TV show, you might say *ég er ekki í stuði*, meaning "I am not in the stuð", which would mean that you just can't muster the enthusiasm to do whatever it is you are required to do.

❖ *Metnaður*

Verbatim translation: there isn't one

Meaning: Sort of like ambition, but not really

Usage: She has put so much metnaður into that performance piece, it's really fantastic.

This is not a sexy word, and probably not all that interesting either, but I *must* be allowed to include it because, in my twenty years of working as a translator, it stumped me every time. The Icelanders use this word a lot. They talk about something being *metnaðarfullt* - full of metnaður. They say this about works of art, or business proposals, or objects that someone has created, or about people. Most translators that are not terribly concerned with nuance (read: not perfectionists, like me) will translate this word as "ambitious" ... but in Icelandic it incorporates far more than that. A person that is *metnaðarfullur* may be ambitious - but the English word denotes something cutthroat, a desire to get ahead. In Icelandic it incorporates a distinct element of quality. In other words, the Icelandic word also includes doing a good job and thereby getting ahead or getting noticed because of the quality, not just because you're prepared to sell out to get attention or to move up in the world. In fact it doesn't even have to denote getting ahead - a work of art can be metnaðarfullt just because someone took painstaking care in its creation, and gave it everything they had, irrespective of whether or not they wanted it to get noticed. Definitely one of the trickier words when it comes to expressing its meaning in English, but also one with many layers of meaning.

Plís

nd now for a word that exists in pretty much every civilised language, but *not* in Icelandic. It is the word... PLEASE.

I am serious. There is no word for "please" in the Icelandic language. The closest we might come to it is, say, *viltu gjöra svo vel*, as in *viltu gjöra svo vel að rétta mér smjörið?* - "would you do so well as to pass me the butter?" Otherwise we simply use *takk*, or "thank you" where English speakers would use "please", as in: "Would you like me to pass you the butter?" "*Já takk.*" (Yes, thank you.)

Meaningless and ubiquitous

If you are around Icelandic-speakers for a while you'll probably start to pick up words that they say all the time and you struggle to make sense of. Words that seem to have a rather nebulous meaning - or sometimes no meaning at all. Every language has them, of course - the English word "well", the German word "also" and the French word "alors" spring to mind. Here are three such examples that are very common in the beloved and gentle.

Jæja

A highly versatile word that can be tricky for those not well versed in the cultural nuances of Icelandic. It can be used to herald in a conversation, as in: *Jæja, það er blessuð blíðan í dag* - "Jæja, the weather sure is nice today". It can also be used as a standalone when a silence becomes uncomfortable - you know, when you don't really know what to say but aren't comfortable saying nothing. The other person would then likely respond *já* - "yes", which would mean nothing except that they heard your jæja and they, too, are feeling kind of awkward.

Jæja can also denote your mood or feeling, depending on the intonation. If the inflection goes up at the end you are probably feeling buoyant and would like to start a conversation in that vein. If the inflection drops at the end you are probably feeling downhearted and pessimistic, and the other person will pick up on this instantly.

Jæja can also be a response to someone who has just told you something fascinating - as in *jæja já!* It can also signal that you want to bring a conversation or exchange to an end. In such an instance you might rise from your seat with a *jæ-ja* that is slightly elongated on the second syllable, and the tone of that jæja would absolutely tell the other person that you think it's time to go.

Heyrðu

The literal translation of this word is "listen" but in Icelandic it is tossed about far more freely than its English counterpart. Heyrðu is most commonly used at the beginning of sentences to command someone's attention. If I were to begin a sentence with "listen" in English it would mean I'm about to say something very important, or to give the other person a piece of my mind. In Icelandic if I used heyrðu I *might* be about to do that, but I might also simply be one of those Icelanders who use it to herald in just about everything they have to say. Example: "So, did you enjoy the concert?"

"Heyrðu, yes!" "Was this your first time seeing this band?" "Heyrðu, no, I saw them last year." "And were they as good back then?" "Heyrðu, yes, they were fantastic." At which heyrðu has plainly become a linguistic tic that is more than a little annoying.

Sko

This is a highly common filler word, that can also be used to give emphasis to something. If a verbal expression is prefaced by sko then it usually means the person is gathering their mental forces to say something magnificent ... or at least something that requires them to gather their mental forces. However, many people pepper every second or third word with sko, particularly if they're stressed out - sort of like "um" in English.

Jú

ere is a word that often confuses our foreign friends: *Jú.* (Pronounced "you".)

Confuses, because when Icelanders say "yes" they will either say já, or jú, and people can't figure out why they sometimes say one, and sometimes the other.

Well, it's simple: já is the correct response to a question formed in the affirmative, and jú the response to a question formed in the negative.

To wit:

"Is this the road to Hurdygurdy*?" Answer: Já.

"Isn't this the road to Hurdygurdy?" Answer: Jú.

* Hurdygurdy is what foreigners who live in Iceland sometimes call the town of Hveragerði.

The quintessential Icelandic words

T hen there are the words or phrases that get to the very essence of the Icelandic national character. Somehow these capture a quirk or quality with which all Icelanders are familiar. They are very much a part of our daily conversations, and while their meaning can be conveyed in English with a sentence or two, there is no corresponding single word that adequately does the job.

Hress

This denotes a state of being or a mental attitude that is buoyant, fun and/or physically robust. If someone asks you how you are doing you might respond with *hress bara!* meaning "feeling good, upbeat, ready to take whatever comes my way!"

Similarly if someone asks how you are but also wishes to communicate that they really don't want to hear about any of your problems, they might say *ertu ekki hress?* meaning "aren't you feeling pretty good?" - to which the expected answer is (naturally): "Jú!"

Meanwhile, if someone has been sick, you might ask them *ertu orðinn hress?* meaning: have you become hress (as in, are you better now)?

Hress can also be used to describe people's character: *Hann er ógeðslega hress gaur*, meaning that, being hress, he is entertaining and fun and will not become excruciatingly annoying while drunk.

Incidentally, the Icelanders place great stock in hress-ness … they like to be hress, they like other people to be hress, and they like to pretend that they are hress even when they are not. Methinks it is a throwback to the old days when the very survival of the community depended on people being hress and not bringing other people down, literally and figuratively. These days, hress is pretty much a requirement for Icelandic citizenship, though no one would actually tell you that. (Except me. You're welcome.)

Nenna

A word the Icelanders say a lot. Basically it means that you cannot be arsed to do something, but with add-ons. The phrase *ég nenni þessu ekki* can mean "I can't be bothered to do this thing because it's boring", or "this thing is so trivial that it is not worth my time", or "I'm lazy so I'm not going to do this thing", or "I don't want to deal with this person's crap" - all depending on the context.

Þetta reddast

If ever there was a quintessential Icelandic phrase *this is it*. Loosely translated it means "it will all work out in one way or another" and the Icelanders normally use it with a delightful combination of laissez-faire and trust in providence. The intrinsic meaning of this phrase is that whoever is stuck with a problem needs to stop obsessing about it and to let it go. Incidentally, this is also a default response when someone tells you about a problem they're having and you don't have a clue what you should say to them. It's sort of a declaration of support, but nuance is of the essence because it could be interpreted as you not really giving a damn. It's a very fine line.

Dugleg/duglegur

A word that is a little hard to pin down. It can be used to describe someone who is hard working, clever, resilient, competent ... or all of the above. You would use it about someone who works hard ("She was really dugleg today, she finished writing five essays"), or a child who does something well (dugleg! - "good job!"), or a dog that does what you want it to (duglegur! - "good boy!"), or someone who is resilient ("she's so dugleg - she goes to the gym every single day") or competent ("he's so duglegur, he took care of all the wedding arrangements single-handedly"). Whatever the use, make no mistake: being dugleg/duglegur is highly prized among the Icelanders.

Ó my

The Icelanders have this curious habit of shortening long words by truncating them somewhere in the middle and slapping an "ó" (pronounced "oh") on the end. There appears to be no rhyme or reason as to why some words are given the "ó" treatment and some are not. Like, say, why the town of Patreksfjörður is colloquially called Patró but its neighbour Tálknafjörður is not called Tálknó. Just as an example.

I sometimes wonder if this "ó" business has grown out of the Icelandic habit of taking things down a notch if they are too formal (because most Icelanders are intensely uncomfortable with anything too formal). Or maybe because it is considered cool in Iceland to be a little bit *kærulaus* (a word that falls somewhere between flippant and careless) and using ó-words is just a little bit *kærulaust*.

Or maybe it just makes the word seem a little more friendly.

Enough philosophising: here are a few of the more common ó-words, along with their origins, literal translation of the Icelandic word (because we love those transparent, put-together words), English translation, and examples of common usage.

Friendly word: *Strætó*
Original word: *Strætisvagn*
Literal translation: Street wagon
English translation: Bus
Usage: Car is on the fritz so I have to resort to strætó, urgh.

Friendly word: *Slysó*
Original word: *Slysavarðsstofa*
Literal translation: Accident protection lounge
English translation: Emergency room
Usage: Fell off my high heels and wound up at slysó for six hours.

Friendly word: *Tengdó*
Original word: *Tengdamóðir / tengdafaðir*
Literal translation: Connected mother/connected father
English translation: Mother-in-law/Father-in-law
Usage: Need a new shirt, have to make a good impression on tengdó.

Friendly word: *Abbó*
Original word: *Afbrýðisamur*
Literal translation: There isn't one
English translation: Jealous
Usage: I went and gave Pétur á hug and now Jón is all abbó.

Friendly word: *Púkó*
Original word: *Púkalegt*
Literal translation: Like an evil sprite or goblin
English translation: Dowdy, uncool
Usage: I'm not wearing those pants, they're so púkó.

Friendly word: *Sígó*
Original word: *Sígaretta*
Literal translation: Cigarette
English translation: Um, cigarette
Usage: I popped out for a sígó and when I came back my phone was gone.

Incidentally, sígaretta is one of those words in the Icelandic language where a new word was made up [*vindlingur*] but it refused to stick. The good folks of the Language Committee had to capitulate to The People on this one.

Friendly word: *Hafró*

Original word: Hafrannsóknarstofnun

Literal translation: Ocean Research Institute

English translation: Marine Research Institute

Usage: Those Hafró scientists are going to slash the cod fishing quota again.

Friendly word: *Skiló*

Original word: *Skilaboð*

Literal translation: Return message

English translation: Message

Usage: Send me a skiló when you get home.

Friendly word: *Saumó*

Original word: *Saumaklúbbur*

Literal translation: Sewing club

English translation: Sewing circle

Usage: The gals loved the cake I made for saumó last night.

Friendly word: *Vandró*

Original word: *Vandræðalegt*

Literal translation: Problem-like

English translation: Awkward, embarrassing

Usage: Accidentally walked in while Jón was on the toilet. Vandró!

Inbreath

This doesn't really count as *language* per se, but I have to mention the Icelanders' quirky way of speaking on the in-breath, especially when they are shocked or indignant. Try saying "Yiiii" while breathing in and you'll get the idea.

And it doesn't have to be only when they're shocked. Some people have *so much to say* and *such a short time in which to say it* that the out-breath just isn't enough; they have to speak while inhaling, too. This is especially true of individuals who want to prevent someone else from getting a word in because that would necessarily halt their verbal onslaught. Simply never stopping to breathe is an excellent strategy for dominating a conversation. Give it a try!

Stressing out

n Icelandic, the stress is always on the first syllable of a word. Always.

This is why, when you hear an Icelander speaking English with a funny accent, chances are that it's not just the harsh tones of Icelandic creeping in but also that they are placing the stress on the wrong part of the word. They will instinctively stress the first syllable unless they know better. For instance they will say *pro*-nunciation, instead of pronunci-*ation*. Or *mis*-understanding, rather than misunder-*stan*-ding.

A couple of exception to this: most Icelanders I have met say Dra-*cu*-la, rather than *Dra*-cula, and o-re-*ga*-no rather than o-*re*-ga-no when they are speaking English. I have no idea why.

The mystery of the missing dialects

One thing that has long puzzled scholars and language nerds about the Icelandic language is the conspicuous absence of dialects. There is not a great difference in the way Icelanders speak from one part of Iceland to another, and what difference there is mainly has to do with pronunciation. Most noticeable is the variation in speech between north and south Iceland - northern Icelanders tend to articulate certain consonants more harshly than their southern countryfolk, in particular p, t and k. They also elongate some of the vowels more than the southerners do.

Now, you might be tempted to assume that dialects did not form because Iceland is small(ish) and sparsely populated. However that alone does not adequately explain it because even in the Faroe Islands, which is a considerably smaller language area than Iceland is, there are dialects.

One theory pertaining to this is that, throughout history, the Icelanders were on the move a lot. The dominant social structure meant that people moved house frequently, and farm labourers changed their situations often. A large share of the population also convened at Þingvellir for a democratic assembly each year. Hence there was a fair bit of interaction between people, and this promoted linguistic regularity. There were no "linguistic pockets" as it were - isolated regions where dialects had a chance to form.

Yet possibly the greatest factor in ensuring uniformity in the language was that the Icelanders almost compulsively wrote things down. They kept records of everything from farm inventory to bloody family feuds. This began very early on and continued throughout the centuries. And once a language is fixed in written form it is subject to far less change than it otherwise would be.

These two factors, plus the aforementioned language purism, are thought to have contributed significantly to the fact that dialects did not develop in Iceland.

Older than our age

And now, a linguistic pet peeve of many an Icelander: the tendency of Icelandic to turn everyone into someone older than they really are.

Let me explain.

In English, if someone is between 20 and 30 years old, you would say they are in their twenties. If they are between 30 and 40 they are in their thirties. And so on.

In Icelandic, if someone is between 20 and 30 you would say *þau eru á þrítugsaldri*, literally "they are in the third-decade age". Granted, that sounds pretty convoluted when translated - it is less so on the original. For instance, when someone is thirty, you would say *hún er þrítug* - "she is three-decades [old]".

But it is not the bizarre wording that bothers people - it is the fact that your age is automatically rounded off to the next decade.

In other words, if someone is one day past their twentieth birthday you would say "they are in the third-decade age" - even if they have a full ten years to go before they hit thirty.

In your twenties this may not be such a big deal. But the higher you crawl up the age ladder, the more annoying it starts to get. Like when you are forty you don't necessarily want it implied that you are fifty. You may be totally OK with ageing and may be doing so with the utmost grace, but you'd probably still much rather be "in your forties". Because that is exactly what you are.

Words for snow

L anguages, as we have established, reflect the daily conditions and realities of the cultures that use them. It should come as no surprise, therefore, that the Icelanders have a whole slew of words to describe certain weather, especially if it involves wind and snow. Being specific about such things was vitally important in the old days when folks had to travel vast distances on foot in all kinds of weather, and their survival depended on how well they were able to assess conditions.

A cursory look at Icelandic words used to describe snow turns up at least sixty. These include terms for freshly-fallen snow (*mjöll*), half-melted snow (*krap*), slushy snow (*slabb*), deep snow (*kafald*), snow where there is a frozen layer on top (*skari*), and an expanse of snow that is hard and frozen (*hjarn*). Snow showers have their own name (*él*), as do snow showers that are so thick that it becomes dark at the same time (*moldél*). Intermittent snowfall has a name (*snjógangur*), as does snowfall with either hail or sleet mixed in (*snjóhraglandi*). Snow with wind is clearly defined (*hríð*), as are the particular variables of that type of snowfall - wet snow with wind (*blotahríð*), light snow with wind (*lenjuhríð*), much snow with wind (*kaskahríð*). Snow accompanied by storm, meanwhile, has a whole separate name (*bylur*), and if it is so thick that you can hardly see in front of you there is a name for it (*blindbylur* or *moldbylur*). Drifting snow has a name (*skafrenningur*), as does drifting snow in light wind (*fjúk*) and drifting snow in heavy wind (*skafbylur*).

My personal favourite snow-related word is *hundslappadrífa*, which literally translates as "dog-paw snowfall". This is the name used for big, wet flakes of snow that drift straight down to the ground when there is no wind and, as it happens, look a lot like the paws of a dog.

Meanwhile, anyone who has been to Iceland will have noticed that the wind is pretty much constant, and often relentless. Small wonder then that Icelandic has over 100 words for wind and windy conditions. These range from words for a light and gentle breeze (*gola*) to a slightly stronger breeze

(*andvari*) to a fresh breeze (*kaldi*) to a strong breeze (*strekkingur*) to storm (*stormur*) to another word for storm (*óveður*) to another word for storm (*mannskaðaveður* - literally "man-harming weather") to another word for storm (*hundaveður* - literally "dog weather" - why I do not know, but presumably because even the dogs wouldn't be set out in it), to rainstorm (*slagveður*), to violent storm (*ofsaveður*), to another word for violent storm (*skakviðri*), to another word for violent storm (*galdraveður* - literally "sorcery storm" - because surely some evil sorcerer must have conjured it up), to another word for violent storm (*músarbylur* - literally "mouse storm" - it's a long story but also has to do with sorcery)... I could go on (and on), but I trust that you get the picture.

Curse it

First of all: PROFANITY WARNING!

o book about the Icelandic language would be complete without a section on curse words.

The Icelandic term for "curse words" is *blótsyrði* (literally *blót*-words). Blót is the ancient word for the pagan celebrations that were held before Iceland adopted Christianity. In those days *að blóta* meant "to worship" or "to sacrifice" whereas today it means, well, to curse.

When the wise chieftain Þorgeir Ljósvetningagoði decided in the year 1000 that Icelanders should convert to Christianity, he also declared that those who so wished should be permitted to *blóta á laun*, or to continue to hold their pagan celebrations in secret. (You will read all about this on page 124.)

Now - surprise surprise - the Christians did not much care for the pagans or their blóts, which they viewed as being tantamount to devil-worship. As a result of this, the strongest curse words in Icelandic came to involve hell or the devil. Also, the word for blót and the word for "curse" became one and the same.

So now, history aside, I give you: the most common Icelandic curse words.

Andskotinn

Translation: The devil

Usage: *Andskotinn, ég gleymdi að slökkva á eldavélinni!*

Translation: The devil, I forgot to turn off the stove!

A slight variation on this is the genitive form *andskotans* meaning "the devil's", which is used pretty much in the same way though it makes no logical sense whatsoever: "The devil's, I forgot to turn off the stove!"

Helvíti

Translation: Hell

Usage: *Helvíti, ég braut tönn!*

Translation: Hell, I broke a tooth!

The same applies here as with andskotinn, in that it can also be used in the genitive: *helvítis*, or "hell's": "Hell's, I broke a tooth!"

Djöfullinn

Translation: The devil

Usage: *Djöfullinn sjálfur!* or *Djöfullinn, ég steig í hundaskít!*

Translation: The devil himself! or The devil, I stepped in dog shit!

Literally speaking, djöfullinn means exactly the same thing as andskotinn, but for some reason it is a marginally stronger curse word. It is used variously by itself, with the reflexive pronoun after it, or to herald in verbal ejaculations, as above. Incidentally, andskotinn can be substituted for djöfullinn in all the above constellations, but helvíti cannot. A variation on djöfullinn exists in the form of djöfulsins, meaning "the devil's".

When the Icelanders want to intensify their curses they simply put one or more of those three words together into one exclamation, as in: *andskotans helvítis djöfulsins!!!* When someone does that, it means something seriously appalling has gone down.

Incidentally, there is also *fjandinn*, or *fjandans*. It also means "the devil" and can be substituted for both andskotinn and djöfullinn, but it is slightly milder than both of those. Also, you would never include fjandinn in the unholy trinity andskotans helvítis djöfulsins. It is simply not of the same calibre of expletive.

The non-blasphemes

Meanwhile, in the non-blaspheme category we have the insults, which are not exactly the same as the blótsyrði, or curse words, as they are generally aimed at a particular individual, or individuals.

Against women (mostly):

Tussa = one of two Icelandic variations on the c-word in English, the other being *kunta*.
Tík = bitch
Hóra/mella = whore
Drusla = slut (once meant "slovenly" but the meaning has changed).
Belja = cow (often used to insult someone who is overweight).

Against men (mostly):

Skíthæll = literally "shitheel", meaning something like "piece of shit".
Drullusokkur = literally "mud sock" or "muddy sock", which also happens to be the term for toilet plunger.

Kúkalabbi = literally "shit walker" (seriously), but means something like "shithead".

Asni = literally "donkey" (corresponding to the insult "ass" in English - not to be confused with "asshole").

Fífl = idiot

Fáviti or hálfviti = half-wit, or imbecile.

Aumingi = literally "weakling", but means "loser". Bizarrely it can also be used to denote sympathy, as in *aumingja þú!* meaning "poor you!".

In addition to the above, "fuck" has been making steady inroads into the Icelandic language in the last few years. I guess devil worship just doesn't pack the same punch as it used to, leading the Icelanders to borrow words so they can amp up the profanity. Like other neologisms that have informally worked their way into Icelandic it has become phonetically adapted, and is written (and spoken) *fokk*. In 2008, when the Icelandic economy came crashing down and the Icelanders took to the streets in protest, one cardboard picket sign with the words HELVÍTIS FOKKING FOKK scrawled in handwriting across it became an emblem for the entire crisis. Somehow those words captured the mood of the nation better than any devil-worshipping blaspheme ever could.

Two stories

Some words have wonderful narratives attached to them. Now, I cannot attest to whether or not these are absolutely, unequivocally true, but I can tell you that I did not make them up. They were told to me. And now I am telling them to you. Because, veracity aside, they're great stories, and I really hope they're true

1. THE STORY BEHIND PEYSA

Peysa

Pronounced: P-eh-sa (think of the way Canadians say "eh")
Meaning: sweater/jumper/cardigan

IN THE OLD DAYS there were some French sailors who fished off the coast of Iceland, especially the East Fjords. They regularly came ashore looking to trade stuff, and one of the things they wanted to have was Icelandic sweaters. My educated guess is that they were sometimes cold and needed something to keep them warm (I won't elaborate on the fact that there exists a strain of dark-haired, brown-eyed people from the area that trace their ancestry back to those French sailors. You can make of that what you will). Anyway, such sweaters could usually be purchased from the farmers in the area, and the sailors would point to the sweaters of the Icelanders they encountered and say "paysan ... paysan" which in French means "farmer" or "peasant". The Icelanders, however, thought they were referring to their sweaters and started calling them *peysan*, or "the sweater". And that is why today we call a sweater (or jumper, to you UK folk) peysa in Icelandic.

2. THE STORY BEHIND KLÓSETT

Klósett
Pronunced: Chlo-sett
Meaning: toilet

THE PROPER ICELANDIC NAME for toilet is *salerni*. During WWII British soldiers occupied Iceland and, probably having heard alarming stories of turf houses, chamber pots, lice and so on, they brought portable latrines with them. The Icelanders had never seen such contraptions, but being Icelanders they were totally open to new things and had no problem making use of them. On the inside of the door there was a lever with which to lock it, and when it was down it read CLOSED. The Icelanders, being used to phonetic spelling, pronounced the word "kloh-sedd", with every letter voiced. According to the story, the bastardisation of the word "closed" gradually morphed into *klósett*, which the Icelanders took to be the name of the contraption, and which most people use to refer to the WC today.

Useful phrases

A nd now, here are a handful of phrases that may come in handy at some point if you're hanging out with Icelanders. They tend to use these a lot.

Takk fyrir síðast

Verbatim translation: Thank you for the last time

Usage: What two Icelanders say to each other after having spent an enjoyable time the last time they met up. "Hæ! Takk fyrir síðast!" one Icelander might say to the other when they meet on the street, to which the most common reply will be: *Sömuleiðis!* meaning "Same to you!" Mind you, this presumes that they actually *did* have fun the last time they met - or at least that they are pretending they did.

Takk fyrir mig

Verbatim translation: Thank you for me

Usage: What you say when you want to thank someone for something that they have done for you, and you have enjoyed. For instance when you are leaving a dinner party, or when someone has given you a gift.

Takk fyrir matinn

Verbatim translation: Thank you for the food

Usage: What you say when you get up from the table after eating a meal that someone else has prepared. Takk fyrir mig also works just as well in that situation.

Verði þér að góðu

Verbatim translation: May it do you good

Usage: This is the most common response to takk fyrir mig or takk fyrir matinn, and therefore what your hosts will likely say when you have thanked them. It is also something that people will say when they enter a room where someone is eating a meal, and/or if they get up to leave the table before others at the table have finished eating.

Ég elska þig

Literal translation: I love you

Usage: Speaks for itself, though please familiarise yourself with the next section before you start using it. Knowledge is power.

Guð hjálpi þér

Literal translation: God help you

Usage: The Icelandic version of "bless you" - what you say when someone sneezes. (Not to be confused with the Icelandic *bless* - "goodbye".) Like the English bless you it originated during the time of the plague, when sneezing was one of the first symptoms of infection. In effect, bless you was a prayer said in the hopes that the person would regain health. In Iceland, if someone sneezed more than three times, the Guð hjálpi þér would be supplemented with *andskotinn missi þig*, meaning "may the devil miss you", since that number of sneezes did not bode well. However, that phrase has fallen into disuse now, probably parallel to the improvement in medical care.

The problem with love

S o as we know, the influx of English is having a considerable effect on the Icelandic language - as it probably is on most of the world's languages.

One noticeable example is that of expressions taking root in the language that are very obviously direct translations of common English sayings, and that don't always fit with proper linguistic conventions. Expressions like *Eigðu góðan dag!*, the literal translation of "Have a nice day!" - a saying that has become increasingly ubiquitous and that makes a certain share of the Icelandic population recoil in horror at the bastardisation of their very own beloved and gentle.

Another problematic word that, according to some, has become more and more intrusive, is the word *elska*, or "love". Or, well, not the word *per se*, but rather its use. The younger generation in particular now elska anything from a good TV show, to pizza, to kittens, to the latest app for their phones. Besties will coo to each other *elska þig!* or transcribe its original source *lovjú!* when they express their affection, or comment on each other's Facebook posts. All of which grates the language purists to the bone.

You see, the word elska is rather more exclusive in Icelandic than in English. The expression "I love you" - *ég elska þig* - has traditionally been reserved for use between lovers. Only lovers. Before it became the Icelandic substitute for the English "love" and was bandied about equally freely, elska denoted romantic, erotic love. You would not, in the good old days, have used that word for anyone who was not your lover. If you wanted to express your love for, say, your children or your parents, you would have said *mér þykir vænt um þig*, which essentially means "I care deeply for you".

But for the generation that has been steeped in English from birth, this vænt um þig business is far too distant and reserved. And, you know, maybe they have a point. We know that the Icelanders of old were fearful of expressing deep emotion because grief and loss were a constant in their lives. However, times have changed, and nowadays people do not routinely die of illness, accident, in childbirth, or whatever. You might say that it has become safer to love. So perhaps the adoption of the English word "love" makes perfect sense in our day and age, language purism notwithstanding.

Family relations

Icelanders tend to be fanatically precise when it comes to describing family connections. It is not enough to say, for example, "this is my uncle" or "this is my niece". That doesn't tell a typical Icelander anything. Instead, if referring to your uncle you would have to say "this is my _____":

> ***móðurbróðir*** = mother's brother
> ***föðurbróðir*** = father's brother
> ***móðursystir*** = mother's sister
> ***föðursystir*** = father's sister

The above refers to an aunt or uncle that is connected to you by blood. Icelandic does not have an "aunt and uncle" term for the spouse of your mother's brother, or the spouse of your father's sister. In that case it would simply be "my mother's brother's wife", "my father's sister's husband", or similar.

As for niece, or nephew:

> **systursonur** = sister's son
> **bróðursonur** = brother's son
> **systurdóttir** = sister's daughter
> **bróðurdóttir** = brother's daughter

That being said, Icelandic *does* have an all-inclusive term for relatives, irrespective of the specific relation: *frændi*, for a male relative, or *frænka*, for a female relative. This term does not care if it is your mother's brother, your second cousin, your third cousin once removed, your nephew, your niece. If it is a blood relative, this term will do the trick to convey the fact that you are related.

Your children, of course, are just your son or daughter. When it comes to grandchildren, however, you need to get specific. Your granddaughter is not simply your granddaughter, but your *dótturdóttir* (daughter's daughter) or your *sonardóttir* (son's daughter). Your grandson would be your *sonarsonur* or *dóttursonur*. You can, however, refer to your grandchildren as your *barnabörn* - your children's children - if you are referring to them in bulk, or in the rare case when you don't want or need to be specific about gender or relationship you might refer to the child as your *barnabarn* - your child's child.

As for in-laws ...

The parents of your spouse are your tengdamóðir ("connected mother") or tengdafaðir ("connected father"). Your spouse's siblings, though, are not your "connected brother" or "connected sister". In that case Icelandic has a special word: *mágur* or *mágkona*.

Confused?

OK: I have a sister named Ásdís. She has a husband named Stefán. Stefán is my mágur because he is male.

I have a brother named Arnar. He has a wife named Íris. Íris is my mágkona because she is female (*kona* means woman).

Also ...

I am married to Erlingur. Erlingur has a brother named Gísli. Gísli is my mágur.

I am married to Erlingur. Erlingur has a sister named Inga. Inga is my mágkona.

Got it?

But here is where the plot thickens: if you are married to someone and they have a sibling and that sibling has a spouse, there is a special name for that relationship, too. For men it is *svilar*, for women it is *svilkonur*.

Consider:

I am married to Erlingur. Erlingur has a brother named Gísli. Gísli has a wife named Ásthildur. Ásthildur and I are svilkonur because we are married to brothers.

Erlingur is married to me. I have a sister named Helga. Helga has a husband named Ragnar. Erlingur and Ragnar are svilar because they are married to sisters.

I am married to Erlingur. Erlingur has a sister named Inga. Inga is married to a guy named Ingólfur. Ingólfur is my *svili*.

However, I cannot say that Ingólfur and I are svilar or svilkonur (meaning one word for the relationship between the two of us) because we are of the opposite sex. I can only say "Ingólfur is my svili" and he can only say "Alda is my svilkona".

It is mind-bogglingly confusing, I know, and you probably wish you had skipped this section entirely. It's OK. You can tear out this page. We understand.

But before you do ...

Icelandic has a handful of terms for relationships that English does not. To wit:

Mæðgur = a mother and daughter, or daughters. Lóa and her daughter Ugla are mæðgur.

Feðgar = a father and son, or sons. Úlfur and his son Kópur are feðgar.

Mæðgin = a mother and son, or sons. Lóa and her son Kópur are mæðgin.

Feðgin = a father and daughter, or daughters. Úlfur and his daughter Ugla are feðgin.

And finally ...

Probably because of the somewhat, shall we say, *liberal* family structures in Iceland, the Icelandic language has a specific name for the father or mother of your child. As far as I know this is a fairly recent addition to the lexicon, and the insinuation, if someone uses this term, is that the parents of the child are not a couple. The term is *barnsmóðir* or *barnsfaðir*, literally: "child-mother" or "child-father" (or "babymommy" and "babydaddy" if you prefer). So if Gunna says to me: "Jón is my barnsfaðir" I would assume that either Jón and Gunna were never together and the baby just ... happened, or that Jón and Gunna were together (but probably not married) and that they have since split up.

OK, that's it. You can go ahead and tear out this page now.

Idioms and proverbs

I dioms and proverbs provide a unique insight into the soul of a nation. They say so much about a people's history - the heartfelt, the tragic, the monumental, the proud. Icelandic has a vast number of idioms and proverbs that are a direct throwback to our nation's past, especially idioms relating to the ocean, which is such a massive force in our nation's history. Many of them we use all the time without ever giving a thought to their origins. What follows is a random sampling - I hope you enjoy reading about them as much as I did.

IDIOMS WITH UNCLEAR ORIGINS

Proverb: *Hver hefur sinn djöful að draga*
Translation: Everyone has their own devil to drag
Meaning: We all have our own cross to bear

Anyone familiar with the English proverb will understand the meaning of the Icelandic one, because it is exactly the same. Interestingly, though, the English proverb focuses on Christian imagery, whereas the Icelandic one has to do with Satanic imagery. Not sure what that says about the mentality of the Icelandic people, but I have to say that I find the image of someone dragging a devil around vaguely amusing.

Idiom: *Eins og skrattinn úr sauðaleggnum*

Translation: Like Satan out of the sheep's leg bone

Meaning: Unexpectedly, out of the blue

If someone suddenly appeared, especially someone I didn't really want to see, I might say *hann kom eins og skrattinn úr sauðaleggnum*, literally "he appeared like Satan out of the sheep's leg bone". Where the affiliation between a sheep's leg bone and the prince of darkness comes in I could not tell you. However I can tell you that, in the old days, Icelandic children (being impoverished and everything) had no proper toys. Instead they played with sheeps' bones, each of which was assigned a role. The jawbones were the cows, the joints of the legs were the sheep, and the leg bones were the horses. So maybe folks were worried that Satan - being the crafty bugger that he was - would install himself in a sheeps' leg bone when the kids were playing and then suddenly BOO! pop out and scare the bejeezus out of them.

It's just a theory.

Incidentally, the use of this idiom is not confined to people - it is also successfully used to comment on unwanted happenings, as in: "Damn, this huge phone bill comes like Satan out of a sheep's leg bone!"

Idiom: *Sautjánhundruð og súrkál*

Translation: Seventeenhundred and sauerkraut

Meaning: In the really olden days

This idiom does not specifically refer to the 1700s. Neither does it have anything to do with sauerkraut. But for some reason it is used to talk about things that happened at an unspecified time "way back when".

Say I was talking about a movie that was set in a century way before ours but I didn't exactly know when. I might say *myndin gerist sautjánhundruð og súrkál*, literally "the film takes place seventeenhundred and sauerkraut". The person I was talking to would then understand that it happened sometime in the undisclosed past.

This expression has a corresponding one in Danish - they say *attendhundrede og hvidkål*, meaning "eighteen hundred and white cabbage". It is quite possible that the Icelanders borrowed the expression from the Danish (it wouldn't be the first thing), and it would make sense for them to replace white cabbage with sauerkraut since the Icelanders were always desperate for ways to preserve food back in the old days, and pickling was one very common method. Sauerkraut, for those who don't know, is simply pickled white cabbage.

Idiom: *Úti að aka*

Translation: Out driving

Meaning: To be way off base / to be distracted

This expression has nothing to do with actual driving, and I wouldn't even want to venture a guess as to its origins. As for its usage, it means that someone is completely scattered or out of it: *Hún er algjörlega úti að aka*, or "she's completely out driving". I am tempted to draw a parallel here with the fact that the Icelanders are notoriously bad drivers, and generally give little thought to their fellow motorists. Maybe this expression originally came into being as a result of this ... although, on closer reflection, I doubt it. If for no other reason than that the Icelanders are absurdly oblivious to the fact that they are horrible drivers, so would likely never have coined such a phrase.

Idiom: *Að falla eins og flís við rass*

Translation: To fall like a splinter to an ass

Meaning: To fit perfectly

English speakers mention hands and gloves when they want to say that something is a flawless fit. Icelanders talk about a splinter and someone's butt. As for which exact splinter was such a close fit with someone's posterior I do not know - and frankly I'm not sure that I want to. But the idiom is fun.

Idiom: *Að kalla ekki allt ömmu sína*

Translation: To not call everything your grandmother

Meaning: To be a badass

If you say about someone *hann kallar ekki allt ömmu sína* you would be talking about someone who is tough, resilient, *hardcore*. Because obviously if you call everything your grandmother you are a big wuss.

No one really knows where this idiom comes from, but there is a theory. Some dude was probably bragging about his ancestors or lineage (as you do), and some (other) wise guy made the sarcastic quip: "He doesn't call everything his grandmother." In other words: "This snob doesn't call everything his grandmother, only the grandmothers worth bragging about." Clearly this resonated enough with the Icelanders to become a permanent fixture in the linguistic landscape.

Idiom: *Þar hitti andskotinn ömmu sína*

Translation: That is where the devil met his grandmother

Meaning: He met his match

Staying on the subject of grandmothers, this delightful saying effectively means that someone has encountered their equal. However, it is only used when two formidable forces come up against one another - as when someone notoriously ill-tempered meets someone else notoriously ill-tempered. Like, say, if a certain Russian dictator suddenly decided to invade

North Korea and came up against the full wrath of another unnamed dictator, I might remark: "Ha! That's where the devil met his grandmother." I'll leave it up to you to decide which dictator is the grandmother.

Idiom: *Að rekja úr einhverjum garnirnar*
Translation: To unravel someone's intestines
Meaning: To question someone / to catch up

In the old days, the intestines of slaughtered livestock were removed so that they could be used to make food, like sausages and such. First, though, the intestines needed to be unravelled and properly cleaned. Somehow over time this task became synonymous with questioning someone intently - though not necessarily in a negative way. Like if I haven't seen someone in a long time and they come to visit, I might say "come inside so I can unravel your intestines", meaning I would want to know what they've been doing since the last time we met.

IDIOMS RELATING TO THE WAYS OF THE PAST

Idiom: *Kemur af fjöllum*
Translation: Comes from the mountains
Meaning: Doesn't have a clue

This idiom is used when someone is completely clueless about something. Like if someone launched into a discussion with me about Jón and Gunna's new baby and I didn't even know Gunna had been pregnant, I'd say *bíddu bíddu ... ég kem af fjöllum*: "Wait, wait ... I come from the mountains."

This goes back to the old days when people would have to travel vast distances to get someplace, or spend hours or even days searching for their sheep in mountainous regions. They'd get back to the farm and be completely oblivious about what had transpired while they were gone - after all, they had just come from the mountains, where there was no one to inform them of anything.

Idiom: *Áfram með smjörið*
Translation: On with the butter
Meaning: Keep going, persevere

Let's say you're writing a book. And you're really into it and everything, but you have this minor obstacle called chronic procrastination. Instead of nailing your butt to a chair and getting on with it, you wind up whiling away the hours on social media and never getting anything done.

To that person (who is completely separate from this author, I assure you) I would say: Áfram með smjörið, which means JUST WRITE THE DAMN THING ALREADY! but without the all-caps because you normally don't shout this idiom. It's more of a gentle coercion.

The origins, of course, are self-evident. Down on the farm, butter needed to be made, and for the butter to be made the cream had to be churned. Butter, incidentally, was really valuable in the old days in Iceland - so much that it was frequently used as currency. People paid their rent and such in butter, and the wealthier farmers often had piles of the stuff out in the storeroom, stacked high like so many gold bars. Not that áfram með smjörið in contemporary usage necessarily denotes making money - it is simply used when someone needs to buckle down and get something done.

Proverb: *Gakktu hægt um gleðinnar dyr*
Translation: Walk slowly through the door of mirth
Meaning: Enjoy yourself in moderation

This "moderation" of which I speak usually, if not always, refers to restraint in the use of mind-altering substances. Like if someone I know is going out on the town and I know they're going to tie one on (or "splash from their cloven hooves" as it were - more on that momentarily) I might say to them gakktu hægt um gleðinnar dyr before they leave.

Origins? Well, back in the day there were limited opportunities for people in Iceland to socialise. Farms were generally far apart and weather conditions unpredictable, so get-togethers were rare. The highlight of the week for most people was going to church on Sundays, as much fun as that sounds.

Except when someone decided to hold a dance. This would generally be at one of the larger farms, and folks would come from far and wide to attend, provided they had first gained permission from their masters. (The proletariat in Iceland in centuries past were subject to innumerable restrictions on their freedom.) In fact, being able to go to these events was so important to some farmhands that they had special clauses in their contracts stipulating that they could attend the nearest dance, whenever one happened to be held.

Actually - and here we come to the crux of the thing - these events hardly deserved to be called "dances". Yes there was dancing involved, but these were first and foremost drinkfests riddled with brawling and debauchery. Folks would get plastered and the carousing would get so out of hand that they would crash into the doorframe when they were going in and out of the farmhouse, and frequently *break it* so the whole doorway would collapse. And so a proverb was born: "Walk slowly through the door of mirth."

Incidentally, these shindigs would regularly get so crazy that they were eventually banned by law. Mainly because people's moral compass tended to malfunction, as sometimes happens when the drinking gets out of hand. The most infamous of these soirées was the Jörfagleði, held annually at the farm Jörfi in West Iceland. At one such, nineteen children are reported to have been conceived out of wedlock. As a result dancing in all its forms was quite literally banned in Iceland from the beginning of the eighteenth century to the end of the nineteenth. Apparently the authorities attributed all those loose morals to the physical act of dancing, rather than the alcohol that was ingested at the same time.

Be that as it may, this proverb is still used in colloquial speech today, possibly because the Icelanders' imbibing of "the cheer" has not diminished much over time - although happily our door frames have become sturdier.

Idiom: *Að sletta úr klaufunum*
Translation: To splash from your cloven hooves
Meaning: To have a great time

The English equivalent of this idiom would probably be "paint the town red". In Iceland we say: "I'm going to splash from my cloven hooves."

The origin of this goes back to when the cows were released from the cowshed in the spring. As you probably know the winters in Iceland can be long and severe, so livestock was kept cooped up indoors for months on end. In the spring when they were put out to pasture the cows would be seized by such exorbitant joy that they would begin to jump and thrash around, throwing their hooves up in the air and splashing water, mud, or whatever happened to be on the ground all over the general vicinity.

Today this is used when people go out celebrating and demonstrate similar jubilation as the cows when they are let out of the shed in the spring - though presumably folks are not actually throwing mud and shit around. It's more of an allusion.

Idiom: *Detti mér allar dauðar lýs úr höfði*
Translation: All the dead lice now fall from my head
Meaning: I am very surprised

Conditions of life in Iceland in the old days were lousy. Literally: there were lice everywhere. People slept on straw or brushwood that were a stellar breeding place for lice colonies. Folks routinely had open lesions on their skin from scratching at their bites so hard.

One thing about the Icelanders is that they tend to make jokes in difficult situations - something that has undoubtedly helped them survive all those centuries of hardship. And they made jokes about the lice. The implication of this idiom is that, being surprised, you shake your head in disbelief and all the dead lice in your hair come tumbling down to the nearest horizontal surface.

Today most people have managed to eradicate lice from their heads and living quarters (we'll leave the heads of elementary school children out of this discussion for the sake of simplicity), but the idiom has stuck. We use it when we are completely flabbergasted. Like if someone came along and told me that Taylor Swift was actually the love child of Donald Trump and Sarah Palin I might exclaim: Detti mér nú allar dauðar lýs úr höfði! - "may all the dead lice now fall from my head!" Just as a hypothetical example.

Proverb: *Að pissa í skóinn sinn er skammgóður vermir*
Translation: Peeing in your shoe won't keep you warm for long
Meaning: Don't look for short-term solutions

Back in the old days, the Icelanders would sometimes have to travel long distances in extreme weather, in clothes that didn't offer a whole lot of protection from the cold. Their footwear, in particular, was hopelessly inadequate: slipper-like shoes made of sheepskin that were so thin that they lasted only a few miles. Practically every story that describes an Icelander setting out on a trip notes that they took with them *nesti og nýja skó*, literally "provisions and a new pair of shoes" - a *spare* pair of shoes, that is, to replace the pair that would inevitably fall apart before long.

Those thin shoes were put on over knitted socks, and the whole caboodle would generally be wet before you were even out of the farmyard. Hence you can imagine how cold people's feet got, say, if there was frost and snow on the ground. On such occasions it might have been tempting to do a little wee in your shoe just to warm your feet - but alas, as we know, you would have been considerably worse off in the long run.

Today we use this idiom for instances when people do something idiotic that they think is going to help in the short term, but will definitely be a major setback in the long term. Like, say, a government making a deal with a big multinational aluminium company to build a brand-new smelter that will initially provide jobs and such but in the long run will just pollute the landscape, kill your rivers, use up all your resources, and not provide any sustainable revenue for the nation. That is a classic case of "pissing in your shoe". Nice and aaaaahh when you first do it, but pretty darn nasty a few minutes later.

Idiom: *Blindur er bókarlaus maður*

Translation: Blind is the man who has no books

Meaning: If you don't have books, you're blind (in a figurative sense, obviously, because if you were blind you couldn't read them anyway).

This idiom pretty much speaks for itself, but allow me to elaborate all the same. As you may know, books are a massive deal in Iceland. The literary tradition hails back to the days when the Icelanders sat in their turf huts and scribbled things down by the light of their fish oil lamps, or read things to each other to pass the time while they were cooped up during those cold, dark winters. Despite the abject poverty in which people lived, illiteracy was virtually unheard of in Iceland all through the centuries. Icelanders cling with a desperate sort of pride to this part of their history (it helps offset the stories of deprivation and squalor), and books and the people who write them are highly revered in Icelandic society to this day. Hence this idiom, extolling the virtue of books.

A variation of this expression is *Betra er brókarlaus en bókarlaus að vera*, meaning "it is better to be without trousers than without a book". Granted, I have yet to see an Icelander wandering around the streets reading a book without trousers on, but that day may still come, who knows.

Idiom: *Að vera með nefið ofan í hvers manns koppi*

Translation: To have your nose in every man's chamber pot

Meaning: To be nosy

Most people probably get the gist of this idiom, which falls squarely into the WTF? category of Icelandic sayings. Seriously: to go around smelling other people's chamber pots? What the hell for? It's not like it's going to provide you with any sort of information, unless you are particularly concerned with your neighbour's bladder or bowel movements. Or if you are a dog.

Equally strange: this idiom is in fairly common circulation today. I cannot think of any reason for why it is so often used, except that it is so freaky.

Idiom: *Heimskt er heimaalið barn*

Translation: Stupid is a child raised at home

Meaning: You stay stupid and closed-minded if you don't expand your horizons.

This idiom, while not really in common use any more, is closely related to the term heimskur, meaning "stupid". *Heimskur* is derived from the word *heima*, which means "home". So the word "stupid" in Icelandic literally means, "he who has never left home".

Which just about says all that needs to be said on that subject.

Idiom: *Ekki eins og fólk er flest*

Translation: Not like most people are

Meaning: Odd, unconventional

I am not sure if this counts as an idiom, but it is certainly a stock phrase used frequently in Icelandic when talking about someone who does not conform to convention. *Hún er ekki eins og fólk er flest* - "She is not like most people are," the Icelanders will say with a hint of derision for the person who dares to buck the system.

For me, it clearly illustrates the tremendous social pressure in Iceland to be eins og fólk er flest - uniform, homogeneous, conforming to the social norms. Something that may have helped the Icelanders survive during times of adversity, but which today is more than a little provincial and, well, *heimskt*.

Idiom: *Hvalreki*

Translation: Beached whale

Meaning: Windfall

As I have already mentioned on one or ten occasions, folks in Iceland used to be poor. *Really* poor, like starvation-poor, especially near the end of winter. And so, one of the most fantastic things that could happen was if a whale washed up on shore. One beached whale could feed a single household for an entire winter, or an entire district for several days. It was an awesome boon in a world where the struggle for survival was frequently desperate.

It was so fantastic, in fact, that the word hvalreki is still very much a part of the Icelandic lexicon, and is used to mean "windfall". For instance let us say that my country (Iceland) was in the midst of a severe economic crisis. Suddenly a volcano beneath a glacier erupts in the most spectacular, photogenic manner - and not only that, but it also stops air traffic across the Western Hemisphere for several days, disrupting everyone's travel plans and generally throwing a massive wrench into the workings of the world. Consequently this country gets put onto the global map in a Big Way, and pictures of it go viral. Everyone suddenly wants to visit Iceland to see the glory with their very own eyes, and the economy bounces back in a way that stuns and amazes everyone. Meanwhile, the Icelanders turn to each other and remark happily *þetta eldgos var algjör hvalreki!*, literally "that eruption was a total beached whale!".

IDIOMS CONNECTED TO SIGNIFICANT EVENTS

Idiom: *Að leggjast undir feld*
Translation: To lie down under a hide
Meaning: To meditate carefully on something
Iceland has the oldest existing parliamentary assembly in the world: the Althing (Icelandic: Alþingi), dating back to 930 AD. In those days folks from all over the country gathered at

Þingvellir, literally "parliament plains", to hold a convention and vote on new laws. Now, in the year 1000 there was a bit of a crisis on the plains (understatement) when a simmering feud between the pagans and the growing number of Christians in the country threatened to erupt. Each side had its own law speaker, and refused to acknowledge the legislation of the other. With the situation about to dissolve into chaos (read: folks posed to chop each other's heads off), someone made the wise call to ask the chieftain Þorgeir Ljósvetninga-goði to act as mediator, as he was highly respected by people on both sides of the dispute. He agreed to take on the job, on the condition that both sides would abide by his decision once he made it.

So old Þorgeir went off and *lagðist undir feld*, literally: laid down under a hide - probably a blanket of some sort, made of animal skin - to meditate on his decision. He stayed there for "a night and a day", and then emerged to say that he considered the most sensible course of action to be for the Icelanders to adopt Christianity. The pagans, on the other hand, could still hold their celebratory feasts (called blót - see the chapter on blótsyrði, page 88), as long as they did so discreetly.

Today if someone was prompting me to make a big decision I might say: *Ég þarf að leggjast undir feld*, or "I need to lie down under a hide". Which would not mean that I was going to lie down for a snooze, but rather that I needed to weigh my options carefully.

Incidentally, Þorgeir Ljósvetningagoði converted to Christianity himself after making his decision, and on returning home to the north of Iceland threw his idols of the Norse gods into a nearby waterfall. That waterfall, which is regarded as one of the most beautiful in Iceland and which many visitors to the country will know, became known as Goðafoss - the Waterfall of the (Norse) Gods.

Idiom: *Að launa lambið gráa*
Translation: To pay (someone) back for the gray lamb
Meaning: To get even

If I was really pissed off at someone and hell-bent on revenge, I might clench my fists and mutter under my breath "I will pay him back for the gray lamb!".

This rather bizarre idiom hails from one of the Icelandic Sagas, called *Heiðarvíga Saga*, or *The Saga of the Heath Slayings*. In it, a dude named Styr kills a farmer named Þórhallur. To Styr this is not a big deal because he has given Þórhallur's son Gestur a gray lamb by way of compensation, so he figures they are even. The only problem was that this gray lamb was a sickly little thing, and did not thrive. Now, I'm going to go out on a limb and guess that Gestur did not consider this poor grey lamb an adequate replacement for his father, so one day when Styr was sitting at his table eating his dinner Gestur crept up behind him and drove an axe into his head. And so the saying "to pay him back for the gray lamb" became a thing ... although why it was not "to pay him back for murdering his father" I do not know.

Proverb: *Enginn verður óbarinn biskup*
Translation: No one becomes a bishop without being beaten
Meaning: To be successful you have to pay your dues
Judging by this you might think that bishops were routinely beaten up in Iceland in the old days. This was not so ... but this proverb may have its origins in a story. Seems there was a bishop named Guðmundur who was always called Guðmundur the Good. He was a tad unruly as a child (read: he was a normal child) and so he was *barinn til bóka* by his elders, literally "beaten to the books" - beaten so that he would study properly. This clever strategy appears to have worked on Guðmundur since he did manage to become a bishop, which was one of the highest social positions in the Iceland of old. For whatever it is worth.

Idiom: *Að tefla við páfann*

Translation: To play chess with the pope

Meaning: To go to the toilet to take a poop

The Icelanders do not go to the toilet to defecate. They go to play chess with the pope.

Now, you may wonder, as I did, what the pope did to get dragged into people's business on the bog. No one really knows, but there is a theory that seems moderately plausible. In the 16th century AD, Iceland switched from being basically Catholic to being basically Lutheran, when in true pious fashion the Lutherans chopped the heads off the last Catholic bishop and his two sons. Afterwards, anything to do with Catholicism was strictly pooh-poohed (see what I did there?) and this expression is thought to have come about because it showed disrespect for the pope. An explanation that I am totally prepared to buy, though I cannot for the life of me understand how the game of chess entered the equation.

Today this expression is nothing more than a funny euphemism for heading to the loo, and most people probably use it without suspecting that it has something to do with the Icelandic Reformation of 1550. Incidentally, it does have a couple of variations: *Að heimsækja páfann* (to visit the pope), *að tala við páfann* (to talk to the pope) and *að gjalda páfanum skatt*

(to pay your taxes to the pope - your poop, presumably, being your taxes). To say nothing of *að taka hraðskák við páfann*, "to play a game of speed chess with the pope", which - you probably guessed it - means to pee.

Idiom: *Að fara hamförum*

Translation: To shape-shift

Meaning: To go ballistic

In Icelandic and Norse mythology there existed a belief that some folks or deities were shape-shifters. Reportedly they could morph into animals or beasts, as in a man transforming into a werewolf, and thereby gain some kind of superpower. They who could do this were said to be *eigi einhamr*, meaning "not of one skin", or shape. The *hamr* (today written *hamur*) was the skin, and this process of changing shape was called að fara hamförum, or "to move from one shape to another".

Today we use this idiom about someone who becomes suddenly angry or violent. We'll say: Hann fór hamförum, "he shifted shape", meaning he went berserk. Occasionally this is also used for someone who is thoroughly industrious, as in "he shifted shape cleaning his apartment last night". If only I could commission a werewolf to clean MY apartment *sigh*.

Idiom: *Að koma fyrir kattarnef*

Translation: To get (someone) in front of a cat's nose

Meaning: To take someone down

If I wanted to kill someone or make them disappear (... I don't, this is just hypothetical) I would probably adopt my most pugnacious, aggressive stance and shout: "I'M GOING TO GET YOU IN FRONT OF A CAT'S NOSE, SUCKER!"

Because then the cat would kill the person, right?

Well, you would think that was the general idea behind this idiom. But it turns out that some academics have formed actual theories about it (in contrast to the armchair theories of the person writing this, who would definitely have gone with the cat idea). One is as follows: There was this fella nicknamed Höttur who lived in seventeen hundred and sauerkraut and who went around terrorising the general populace He was a bloody assassin of the worst sort, and had butchered a whole bunch of folks, including the Queen of Denmark. Now, it seems that a certain idiom was popular in the 17th century: *Að koma fyrir Hattar nef*, or "to get someone in front of Höttur's nose". The more astute among you will have realised that Hattar and kattar are very similar - so similar, in fact, that it is easy to imagine the "h" being replaced by "k" over time, especially after old Höttur had exited the stage and his celebrity faded from popular culture. At which time people probably thought that their forebears had been saying that idiom wrong for all those years: "Hahaha, they said *höttur* all the time, when the correct form was *köttur*, hahaha!" but of course THE JOKE IS ON THEM.

MODERN IDIOMS

Idiom: *Ég sel það ekki dýrar en ég keypti það*
Translation: I'm not selling it dearer than I bought it
Meaning: I take no responsibility for its validity
This idiom, translated into English, sounds a tad clumsy, or at the very least old-fashioned. In Icelandic it rolls ever-so easily off the tongue, which may be why people use it so often. It is something you would say when you're relating a piece of information but you're not sure how true it is. As in, "I heard that people actually have sex in the Blue Lagoon, but I'm not selling it dearer than I bought it". That tells the other person that you're not entirely sure about the validity of the story, but that it sounds plausible enough for you to tell them about it.

Idiom: *Að taka í bakaríið*
Translation: To take someone to the bakery
Meaning: To scold someone, to give them a thrashing
This idiom has nothing to do with bread, or cakes, or pastries. It means to whoop someone's butt, literally or figuratively, as in, "Those Mets really took them Dodgers to the bakery, man!"

No one really knows how or why this expression originated,

but there is speculation that it may have morphed from the colloquial expression *að baka* (to bake) something, which in some contexts means "cause". For example *að baka vandræði* literally translated means "to bake trouble" but actually means "to cause trouble". Which is as good an explanation as any because, Lord knows, it is hard to imagine just what bakeries have to do with someone getting their butt kicked.

Idiom: *Að leggja heilann í bleyti*
Translation: To soak your brain
Meaning: To ruminate on something

If someone asked me to come up with an outstanding Icelandic name for "outlet" or "wannabe" or "casual", I would probably say, "Hm. I'll have to soak my brain". This would mean that I planned to think it over and come up with something brilliant.

Apparently this idiom draws its meaning from the fact that anything fertile tends to be wet. I guess it means essentially the same thing as *að leggjast undir feld*, but without the monumental historic connection.

A variation of this is *að leggja höfuðið í bleyti* - "to soak your head", which is more or less interchangeable with the brain soak.

Idiom: *Uppi á þér typpið*

Translation: Your dick is up

Meaning: You're feeling pretty good about yourself

If someone is feeling very pleased with themselves about something, especially if it is something vain or silly, you might say *aldeilis uppi á þér typpið í dag!* literally: "Your dick sure is up today!" This idiom gets used a fair bit and is generally spoken in a rather droll manner. Note: you would not say this to your boss, your teacher, or to anyone with whom you are not on toilet-humour terms. Extra droll-points if you say this to a woman, for obvious reasons.

Idiom: *Að skíta upp á bak*

Translation: To shit up onto your back

Meaning: To make a colossal mess of things

This idiom has nothing eloquent or poetic about it. It does not have a back story (unless you count the back referred to in the idiom itself, hehe). It simply describes what might happen if a baby did a very large number two and its diaper wasn't very snug. Also, this idiom gets used a lot. Maybe because we have had so many instances lately of our politicians shitting up onto their backs in the most outrageous manner. So, yeah. This idiom is frequently used about politicians, or anyone who just keeps getting themselves deeper and deeper into the quagmire of their own upfuckery.

Idiom: *Of seint í rassinn gripið*

Translation: The ass has been grabbed too late

Meaning: An opportunity has passed you by

No one seems to know where this rather, er, unconventional expression comes from. I have read something about it potentially having something to do with the 17th-century idiom *að grípa í rassinn á deginum*, literally "To grab the ass of the day" meaning "to start something too late". Which does not sound like a very believable explanation, given that the last time I checked "the day" didn't have "an ass", or any other body part for that matter.

I have also read speculation about this being about an attempt to save a drowning man by grabbing at him. *Really?* I mean, how many of us would grab someone's *ass* if that person was drowning? Surely an arm or a leg or even a handful of hair would yield better results if your objective was to save someone.

Be that as it may, this idiom gets a fair bit of traction today. Like if your best friend wanted to go to the mall to check out the sales and it was already three weeks since they started you might say *ég held að það sé of seint í rassinn gripið*, literally: "I think it's a little too late to grab the ass." That would mean you think all the good stuff is gone already.

Idiom: *Að skjóta ref fyrir rass*

Translation: To shoot a fox past an ass/instead of an ass

Meaning: To trick someone, to be quicker than someone

Another "ass" idiom, and another one with no clear origins. To complicate things further this particular saying allows for two different interpretations in Icelandic. It could mean "to shoot a fox *past* an ass" (as in bypassing someone's butt), or it could mean "to shoot a fox *instead of* an ass" (as in: the bullet was intended for someone's butt, but it accidentally shot a fox instead). So when translating this idiom it is a little difficult to know which interpretation is right because the origins are not clear, and neither do we know what the person who coined it was thinking. Or *not* thinking. Because maybe they were high.

As to educated guesses about its humble beginnings, all I could find is that it could be about hunting, more specifically about someone shooting a fox past the butt of someone else who lay in wait for it. In other words the owner of the butt was outwitted by the shooter, who claimed the prize of shooting the fox even though the other guy was lying in wait.

Today someone might use this idiom, say, when they see someone heading for the last parking space in the lot and manage to slip in there ahead of them, stealing it from under their nose. They would probably chuckle under their breath and say smugly to themselves: "Hehe, I shot him a fox past a butt," while steadfastly ignoring the rage being hurled in their direction.

IDIOMS CONNECTED WITH THE SEA

Idiom: *Sjaldan er ein báran stök*
Translation: Rarely is there only one wave
Meaning: Bad luck comes in twos (or more)

Waves on the sea rarely come as single entities. There is usually a small one followed by increasingly larger ones, culminating in a big one. The fishermen of old knew this and counted the waves, knowing exactly when to land their boats. If they failed to land properly they would be hit with a larger and even more powerful wave, possibly crashing their boat into the shoreline and thus destroying it, or becoming sucked back out to sea. Today when the Icelanders want to say something like "when it rains it pours", meaning they're being hit with more than a single bout of bad luck, they say this: "Rarely is there only one wave."

Idiom: *Að koma ári sinni vel fyrir borð*
Translation: To place your oar well over the side
Meaning: To become affluent

In the old days, people rowed out to fish, and if they found a good way of using their oars while rowing they could propel themselves faster and more efficiently. Today we use this idiom about someone who is successful in business. "She managed to place her oar well over the side" means she's done well for herself financially.

Idiom: *Að haga seglum eftir vindi*

Translation: To arrange your sails according to the wind

Meaning: To be flexible, to tackle situations as they arise

When you are out at sea, it is important to be able to work with the elements and arrange your sails in such a way that you a) get to where you are going and b) don't meet with disaster. Today when an Icelander says "I'm going to arrange my sails according to the wind," they are saying they're going to adapt to whatever circumstances are at hand.

Idiom: *Að sigla milli skers og báru*

Translation: To sail between a skerry and a wave

Meaning: To navigate a tough situation

A skerry is a small, craggy rock that juts out of the sea or is submerged just below the surface, depending on the tide. Skerries have always presented problems for fishermen because if your boat crashed into one it could easily put a hole in the bottom. Today if you say "I'll have to sail between a skerry and a wave on this one" it means that you're faced with a tricky situation that demands tact, diplomacy or care, and you have to be judicious about how to handle it.

Idiom: *Að taka of djúpt í árinni*

Translation: To put your oar in too deep

Meaning: To exaggerate

In the past, if you placed your oar deep into the water while rowing you could propel the boat more forcefully than if you put the oar in just below the surface. Today if we say "Aren't you putting your oar in too deep?" we are asking whether that person is saying something a bit over the top in order to increase the impact of their words. Not to be confused with "placing your oar well over the side" which, while ostensibly similar, means something quite different.

Idiom: *Að sitja fast við sinn keip*

Translation: To sit firmly at your oarlock

Meaning: To be inflexible or stubborn

The oarlock is where the oar is fastened at the side of a rowboat. This idiom refers to someone who rowed out to fish regularly as part of a crew and always sat in the same place, refusing to change it up. In our modern usage it means someone who is stubborn or adamant about something, as in: "He insists on believing that elves live in his garden, and he sits firmly at his oarlock."

Idiom: *Að búa svo um hnútana*

Translation: To fix the knots in such a way (that...)

Meaning: To make an arrangement

The fishermen of old placed great stock in good knots. They needed to be tied well so that they would hold. Today we use this expression when we talk about arranging something that needs to work out a certain way. Like if I was expecting Jón to come over and Jón's ex was planning to drop by on the same day and I knew they would be at each other's throats within five minutes, I would fix the knots in such a way that Jón came in the morning and his ex came in the afternoon. Easier for everyone.

Idiom: *Að leggja árar í bát*

Translation: To lay your oars in the boat

Meaning: To give up

If you're out in a rowboat and you stop rowing you know what will happen: you'll be at the mercy of the elements, no longer in control. When the Icelanders want to say something along the lines of "I'm not about to throw in the towel" they say, "I'm not about to lay my oars in the boat". In other words, they're not about to give up.

Idiom: *Að krafsa í bakkann/að klóra í bakkann*

Translation: To scratch at the bank

Meaning: To attempt something difficult or hopeless

This idiom conjures up a fairly dramatic image: someone is drowning and literally scratching at the bank, or the shore, desperate to save themselves. Today when we use this we don't necessarily mean it's a matter of life and death, but more like someone trying to do something that's virtually impossible. Like for instance if Iceland's prime minister did something completely mercenary and self-serving like lowering taxes on the rich (including himself) and handing out fishing quotas to his family and friends, and the masses became furious and threatened to oust him from office and vote in the Pirate Party, and then he went and threw the masses a bone in the form of mortgage debt relief that was basically a ruse because in the end it all got eaten up by inflation anyway, I might say something like: "look at the PM, he's really trying to scratch at the bank". In other words I was pretty sure that he knew he was *going down* and was using some lame trick that everyone saw through to save his sorry ass.

A variation on this saying is *að berjast í bökkum*, or "to fight at the banks" meaning someone is fighting desperately to claw his or her way up the bank. Very similar to the idiom above, except that this one refers exclusively to financial struggles.

As in, "The PM is throwing a bone to the people who are fighting at the banks after the calamity that was the economic meltdown". The English equivalent of this would probably be "to stay afloat financially". Note: "banks" here has nothing to do with financial institutions.

Idiom: *Að vera einn á báti*
Translation: To be alone in a boat
Meaning: To be unsupported

It's a pretty lonely thought, you have to agree: someone sitting alone in a boat, especially if they've laid their oars in it. When we Icelanders want to say that someone is on their own without much support, we say something like: "Gunna is a single mom, and she's totally alone on a boat."

Idiom: *Að lægja öldurnar*
Translation: To ease the waves
Meaning: To try to calm a situation

The imagery evoked by this idiom pretty much explains it. When emotions are running high and someone is trying to calm things down, you would say they are trying to "ease the waves". A corresponding idiom in English would be "to calm the waters".

Idiom: *Að fara á fjörurnar*

Translation: To go to the shores

Meaning: To flirt

"To go to the shores" with someone... meaning to flirt with them? I know. On the surface it makes no sense, and trust me - when most Icelanders think about this idiom they have no clue what it means, either. But it's like this: in centuries past, a whole lot of valuable things might be found down at the seashore. These were things that had been washed ashore by the ocean, especially after a storm. So people would head down there to see what they could find - like maybe driftwood, or something from a shipwreck, or even (hallelujah!) a beached whale. Today when we say someone is going to the shore with someone, it means they are flirting with them - not just casually, but with intent. The implication being that the flirtation might result in something valuable - like them bringing home the man or woman of their dreams. Aw!

Idiom: *Að finna einhvern í fjöru*

Translation: To find someone at the shore

Meaning: To get even, to settle the score

Another "at the shore" idiom, but this one slightly more

ominous. Its origins date way back to when trials over people who were accused of theft were held at the seashore. Apparently this was customary not just in Iceland, but elsewhere in Europe, too. Sometimes executions would also be carried out at the shore if the thieves were found guilty, though it is not known whether this was done in Iceland. At any rate, most people knew the law, and this expression became regarded as a threat. When the law became obsolete the original meaning of the idiom faded from popular awareness, but it nevertheless remains in the language to this day.

Idiom: *Að hafa marga fjöruna sopið*
Translation: To have gulped from many a shore
Meaning: To have lived an eventful life

The implied meaning of this idiom is of a fisherman or sailor who has been shipwrecked a few times and has therefore washed up on many a shore. In Icelandic the term "washed up" has none of the negative connotation that it has in English, though. On the contrary, there is usually an implied awe and respect, as in "Jón once fought a lion in Africa and won, and was abducted by kidnappers in South America but got away. He's certainly gulped from many a shore".

Idiom: *Að draga saman seglin*

Translation: To gather your sails together

Meaning: To downsize

This saying refers to something financial or commercial. If you have a company and you find yourself in a recession, you may have to downsize. In Icelandic you would say you had to "gather your sails together". To weather the storm, as it were. Incidentally, there is always an implied sense here that you do this because you must, not just because you think it is a good idea to reduce the size of your company.

Idiom: *Að hafa aldrei migið í saltan sjó*

Translation: To have never pissed into a salty sea

Meaning: To have limited experience in life

Setting aside for a moment the fact that all sea is salty, this expression is used about someone who has been coddled or spoiled all their life. There is usually a hint of derision in this expression - picture a grizzled old seafarer talking about the son of a rich Danish merchant in the Iceland of old, who comes to foreclose on the seafarer's property because he (seafarer) can't pay off his debt to the merchant. The seafarer would likely spit after him and mutter under his breath, "That one has never pissed into a salty sea". Or possibly something much worse.

Words no longer
in use

In the first half of this book we discussed new words that enter the Icelandic language and that require proper Icelandic names that are supplied by the Language Committee ... but what about words that have become obsolete because the concepts they describe no longer exist? As this book draws to a close, here are a handful of words that hail back to a time way before ours. Some of these have acquired a modern meaning, others have simply turned into linguistic fossils, though most Icelanders will still be aware of what they represent.

Baðstofa

Verbatim translation: Bath lounge

In the old turf farms, the communal living room was the baðstofa, and when I say "living" room I mean literally that - this is where people lived, slept, ate, worked, gave birth, died ... basically did everything a person does in a life. The meaning of the word harks back to the Settlement Age, when Iceland still had forests and people had a fairly easy time of it - they lived in stately longhouses with a number of different rooms, including one room used specifically for "bathing" - which actually meant taking saunas. A couple of centuries after the Settlement, things started to go south (or should that be north?) temperature-wise, when the Little Ice Age hit and it became a lot colder than before. By then almost all the wood that had originally covered Iceland (yes, there were actual forests) had been cut down (those settlers had taken a lot of saunas), so people started to huddle together for warmth. The room that tended to be the warmest was the sauna room, so people gravitated towards it. Gradually, over years and decades and even centuries, everyone moved into one room for warmth - and probably also because they were desperately poor and oppressed and had no means of building better homes. They had long since stopped taking saunas by then, but the name - baðstofa - stuck. Today, of course, the turf farms, and hence the *baðstofur*, no longer exist, but we all know about them. After all, only about a century has passed since people still lived in them.

Kvöldvaka

Verbatim translation: Evening-wake

In the old days, people spent the long dark hours of the Icelandic winter indoors in the baðstofa, doing work like spinning, carding, knitting and making tools. Something had to be done to keep people awake and entertained while they worked, so folks told stories, read aloud from books (for those lucky enough to own books), made up rhymes and verses, and so on. This programme of entertainment was called the *kvöldvaka*, literally "evening wake" (as in, staying awake, not as-in-someone-died wake). The kvöldvaka existed on just about every farm in the country, and in hindsight it was a pretty significant institution - it was where children were taught to read and write, and where they were educated, through the stories and recitals that they heard. The wireless radio effectively killed the kvöldvaka, but the word is sometimes still used to talk about rustic-type entertainment, especially during camping trips or other such outings.

Að guða á glugga

Verbatim translation: To God on the window

Again, this harks back to the baðstofa and the turf farms. In those days, people believed in ghosts and all sorts of other apparitions, and were pretty afraid of them. During the winter it was dark a lot, and those fears and anxieties grew. So when a visitor came to the farm, they did not automatically go to the front door of the farm and knock on the door, but instead went up to the window (which was easily accessible, the roof being made of turf and all) and spoke the words: "Here be God." This would prove to the farm folk that the visitor was of the mortal variety and not a ghost, because ghosts were unable to say the word "God". It was thus safe to go to the front door and open it. This action of someone going to the window and saying *hér sé guð* (here be God) was called "to God on the window" - "God" being the verb.

Ljúflingur

Verbatim translation: Sweet, gentle man

As most people interested in Iceland will know, the Icelanders once believed in a strain of people called *huldufólk* that were invisible to most mortals. (And yes, some folks still believe that these apparitions exist - but not many.) These hidden people, also known as elves, inhabited rocks and hillocks in the landscape, and according to the stories their lives were

infinitely better and more magical than those of the mere mortals. Some of the hidden people folk stories describe relationships between mortal women and hidden men, who were called *ljúflingar*. These were doomed love affairs since the two worlds could never converge, yet the ljúflingar provided the mortal women with the sort of love and kindness that they probably never received in their actual lives. I have elaborated on this in my books *The Little Book of the Hidden People* and *The Little Book of the Icelanders in the Old Days*, and will refrain from doing so here. Suffice it to say that most Icelanders will not associate the term ljúflingur with elves, but rather with its modern meaning: a man who is kind, gentle and generally liked by most people.

Útburður

Verbatim translation: Out-carried (child)

In the Iceland of old there were strong penalties for having children out of wedlock. Regular working folks were not permitted to marry until they had acquired a financial standing that most people could never hope to attain in their lifetime. Given the penalties for illegitimate births, this effectively meant that people were not allowed to have sex until they were old enough to afford it. Yet human nature tends to be stronger than laws and decrees, and consequently births out of wedlock were not uncommon. One theory behind the ljúflingar stories (see above) is that they were made up by women who had become pregnant and who tried to escape punishment by claiming that the father of the child was from the hidden world. I am not sure whether that would automatically lower the penalty, but that is one of the theories. The other solution that many parents (often young mothers) resorted to in desperation, especially since they were not in a position to feed, clothe or even house their young ones, was the one referred to by this word. This solution was so common that it had its own name: útburður, meaning to carry a child outside and leave it there to die.

Niðursetningur
Verbatim translation: Put-downer

Life in old Iceland was incredibly harsh, not only due to extreme climate and abject poverty, but also oppression and control by the state authorities. For instance if the male head of a household died, the powers-that-be would quickly step in, take over the farm, and auction off all its residents' belongings. The remaining members of the household, which usually meant the widow and children, were divided up and sent to various farms in the area to be labourers (even children as young as five years old were put to work). They then acquired the label niðursetningar, meaning a person who has been "put down" somewhere where they don't belong. To add an excruciating twist to an already cruel practice, the money for their "upkeep", paid by the district to the owner of the farm that took them in, accrued as a debt that the "put-down-er" would have to pay back. A terrible practice that is one of the darkest stains on the fabric of Icelandic society, and which unfortunately still carries a stigma in some families. To be a "put-downer" was considered enormously shameful, even if the person in question had done nothing to bring it on themselves.

Sel

Verbatim translation: There isn't one

Meaning: Mountain dairy.

In the old days, in the summer, livestock was usually herded up to mountain pastures. This was done both because the pastures there tended to be more lush than those closer to the farms, and also to preserve the fields near the farms for haymaking. The sel was a rudimentary structure, often only a stack of stones with a makeshift roof, and workers from the farm were sent there for the entire summer. Sometimes it would only be one woman, the *matselja*, or "sel-food-woman". Her job was to milk the sheep twice a day and make *skyr* (Icelandic dairy product, similar to yoghurt) and butter from the milk. It is actually in the sel that many of the stories of the ljúflingar originate. We can surmise that it was pretty solitary up there, and that the stories of the romantic hidden men came about through the fantasies of lonely women who sought solace in their imaginations. Yet a more sinister explanation that has been proposed is that the women who worked in the sel were raped, either by outlaws that roamed the mountainous areas, or (more likely) the farmers or sons of farmers who had them in their employ. In many cases they probably became pregnant, and conceived the tales of the ljúflingar to explain away their pregnancy (see discussion of útburður, above). Be that as it may, the meaning behind the word sel is lost to most modern Icelanders, but it does appear in many modern place names, and even street names - such as Seljavegur.

Slang answer key

Okay then! Here we have the long-awaited answer key to all those words that you were unable to decipher on page 32!

(I am joking, of course. I know you were able to decipher most of them because you are brilliant.)

1. **Bömmer** - bummer
2. **Meika sens** - make sense
3. **Kræst** - Christ (as in Djísus)
4. **Fríkað** - freaky
5. **Dömpa** - (to) dump (someone)
6. **Stöffa** - (to) stuff
7. **Kreisí** - crazy
8. **Sjitt** - shit
9. **Bögg** - (to) bug. Also used as a noun (this is a major *bögg*, read: annoyance).
10. **Deit** - date. Bizzarely this word has made inroads into the Icelandic language, despite the fact that the Icelanders typically do not date (for more on that, check out *The Little Book of the Icelanders*).

11. **Sánd** - sound
12. **Djók** - joke (noun). Also *djóka*, when used as a verb.
13. **Sjokk** - shock
14. **Plís** - please
15. **Djísus** - Jesus (as in Kræst)
16. **Pein** - pain
    (as in: She's a royal pein in the butt)
17. **Sækó** - psycho
18. **Brönsj** - brunch
19. **Gúgla** - to google
20. **Osom** - awesome
21. **Tjilla** - to chill (out)

While some of the above may be used in a number of ways in the original language, in Icelandic the slang term is usually only used in one way. Example: shock, which can be both a noun and a verb in English, would not be used as a verb in Icelandic (to shock someone), but only as a noun (that was a major shock). Conversely dömpa (to dump) would only be used as a verb, and not as a noun (a garbage dump).

Also, when these terms are used as verbs in Icelandic, they are usually tagged with the suffix -a which commonly denotes an Icelandic verb (*hlaupa*/run, *hoppa*/jump, *dansa*/dance, etc.) - hence dömpa, djóka, meika sense, and so on.

Happy and blessed

There are two English words that I have not yet mentioned, both of which have stubbornly installed themselves in the Icelandic language: the greeting *hæ* and the parting *bæ*. (Kindly decipher using my super-duper pronunciation key if you don't quite catch their meaning.)

This ubiquitous pair is a fairly recent addition to the Icelandic lexicon. Like Coca-Cola, nylon stockings and chewing gum they arrived with the US air force in 1940 (ish), and have been around ever since, even though the US forces are long gone.

Mind you, hæ and bæ have not completely managed to replace the traditional greetings. Those are still very much in use today, and I want to mention them here because they are pretty adorable - something we Icelanders tend to forget until foreigners come along and remind us.

In Icelandic, the proper way to greet a woman is *komdu sæl*, and for a man *komdu sæll*.

Which literally means: Come happy.

Similarly, when taking leave of someone we say *vertu sæll*, or *vertu sæl*. Which literally means: Be happy.

These also come with variants, such as *komdu sæll og blessaður* and *vertu sæl og blessuð*, which translates as "come happy and blessed" and "go happy and blessed", respectively.

If I walk into a room where there are several people gathered and want to say hello to everyone at the same time, I might say *sælt veri fólkið*, which means "happy be [you] the people".

The most common Icelandic way of saying goodbye, meanwhile, is *bless*, or sometimes bless bless. The word "bless" means the same thing in Icelandic and English, so bless as a parting essentially means, "be blessed".

Just so we're clear: these are not archaic terms, they are expressions that are commonly used and very much alive in the language today.

And now that we have come to the end of this brief romp through the Icelandic language, let me take leave of you using my very favourite parting phrase:

Bless, bless.

IN CLOSING

If you enjoyed this book, please consider giving it a rating on Amazon, Goodreads, or wherever you share your love of books. This is an independently published project and any help getting the word out is hugely appreciated. Thank you in advance!

For more on Iceland and the Icelanders, and to be notified of any new releases, discounts, and more, please sign up for my monthly newsletter. You can find the sign-up form on my website aldasigmunds.com, and also on my Facebook page facebook.com/AldaSigmundsdottir. I am also on Twitter as @aldakalda and on Instagram as @aldamin, and would love to connect.

ACKNOWLEDGEMENTS

Big, big thanks to all the people who helped me put this project together. To my beta readers Ashley Garcia, Clara Cunha, Peter Schneider, Stephen Cowdery and Vida Morkuna, who all offered invaluable insights and feedback in the early stages of this project. To Megan Herbert, whose grace, humour, resourcefulness and talent makes her the best collaborator I could ask for. To Sarah Larsen, who meticulously read over the manuscript in its final form and helped eliminate all those pesky little errors. To my husband Erlingur Páll Ingvarsson, for his awesome design skills, creative solutions, and all-round love, camaraderie and support. Thank you all!

A special hat tip goes to the Icelandic Web of Science (visindavefur.is), run by the University of Iceland. It contains a wealth of information about virtually anything, including the stories behind many of the idioms in this book.

ABOUT THE AUTHOR

Alda Sigmundsdóttir is a writer, journalist and translator. She was born in Iceland, raised in Canada, and has also lived in Germany, Cyprus and the United Kingdom. She has written extensively about Iceland for the international media and regularly gives talks and lectures about various aspects of Icelandic society. Catch up with Alda on her website aldasigmunds.com, or find her on Facebook, Twitter and Instagram.

Other books by Alda Sigmundsdóttir, available through Amazon or on aldasigmunds.com:

The Little Book of the Icelanders
The Little Book of the Icelanders in the Old Days
The Little Book of the Hidden People
Icelandic Folk Legends
Unraveled - a Novel About a Meltdown
Living Inside the Meltdown

THE LITTLE BOOK OF ICELANDIC
© Alda Sigmundsdóttir, 2016

Little Books Publishing
Reykjavík, 2016

Layout and cover design: Erlingur Páll Ingvarsson
Illustrations: Megan Herbert

ISBN 978-1-970125-06-1

LITTLE BOOKS
PUBLISHING

Printed in Great Britain
by Amazon